NEW
BATHROOM
IDEAS THAT WORK

NEW BATHROOM
IDEAS THAT WORK

SCOTT GIBSON

The Taunton Press

The Taunton Press
Inspiration for hands-on living®

The Taunton Press, Inc.,
63 South Main Street, PO Box 5506
Newtown, CT 06470-5506
e-mail: tp@taunton.com

Editor: Carolyn Mandarano
Copy editor: Nina Rynd Whitnah
Indexer: Cathy Goddard
Interior design: Carol Petro
Layout: David Giammattei
Illustrator: Christine Erikson
Cover Photographers: (Front cover, clockwise from top): © Gridley + Graves, design: Craig Kettles, C designs, www.c-designs.biz; © Dulcie Horowitz; © Eric Roth; © Mark Lohman; © Eric Roth; (Back cover, clockwise from top): courtesy of The Kohler Co.; © Tria Giovan; © Tria Giovan; © Ken Gutmaker; © Mark Lohman; © Karen Melvin

Library of Congress Cataloging-in-Publication Data
Gibson, Scott, 1951-
   New bathroom ideas that work / Scott Gibson.
        p. cm.
   Includes index.
   ISBN 978-1-60085-357-9
1. Bathrooms–Remodeling. I. Title.
   TH4816.3.B37G533 2012
   690'.42--dc23
                                        2011049360

Printed in the United States of America
10 9 8 7 6 5 4 3 2 1

The following names/manufacturers appearing in *New Bathroom Ideas That Work* are trademarks: BioGlass℠, BioLet®, Eco-Top™, EnviroSLAB™, Halogená®, Hatbox®, IceStone℠, Nuheat™, PaperStone®, Schluter®, Schluter®-Ditra, Vetrazzo®

ACKNOWLEDGMENTS

This book would not have been possible without the architects, designers, and other professionals who graciously took time to participate. Thanks to Debbie Wiener, Mary Jo Peterson, Erica Westeroth, Alan Asarnow, Rosemarie Rossetti, Terry McKeown, Cynthia Liebrock, David Wagner, Debbi Cleary, Eliza Hart, Jean Larsen, Amy Blackstone and Krieger + Associates, Julia Zander and Russ Hamlet, Maraya Droney, Rick Skalak, Anne Callender, John Whipple, Belinda Marzi, and Terry McKeown of Ulrich Inc.

To the many photographers whose work is represented in these pages, thank you. Bathrooms are not the easiest spaces to photograph.

At The Taunton Press, my thanks and appreciation to Carolyn Mandarano, the editor of both this book and the first edition of *Bathroom Ideas That Work* in 2007, and Katy Binder, the photo editor. Thanks also to the able design and production staff at Taunton, people who always make the most of the material they are given and whose extra efforts are truly appreciated.

CONTENTS

INTRODUCTION

The first edition of *Bathroom Ideas That Work* was published in 2007, and since that time, there have been two significant changes in the world of residential construction. First, the bottom fell out of the U.S. housing market; second, green building has become much more widely practiced. Both of these have changed the way we look at bathroom design.

The painful contraction of the housing industry has meant fewer construction jobs and lower property values for many homeowners. That, no doubt, has discouraged many people from selling their homes until the market improves. At the same time, the situation has provided an incentive for homeowners to repair and renovate what they already have.

According to the 2011 cost vs. value study published by Hanley Wood's *Remodeling* magazine, a midrange bathroom remodel will earn back 64 percent of its cost at resale. An upscale remodel returned only 57 percent. That suggests money for bathroom additions and renovations should be spent wisely, not on trendy upgrades but on high-quality building materials and fixtures that will hold their value.

The other development has been the rise of green building, a much different way of looking at design and construction than in the past. Among the most important values of green building is sustainability, which puts a special emphasis on conserving water, energy, and other natural resources. For a variety of reasons, conservation is becoming a practical necessity for many of us. Supplies of clean water are under increasing pressure in some parts of the country and will continue to be in high demand for agriculture, recreation, and industry as well as houses. The same can be said of energy that's used to heat and cool our homes—it's more expensive and harder to get. There are, however, many bathroom products on the market that save significant amounts of water or energy without sacrificing creature comforts. You simply need to ask the right questions before making a product selection.

Resource conservation also encourages the use of durable building materials, especially those that can be found locally. How does this drive bathroom design? By putting a premium on fixtures and materials that don't have to be replaced often. What this means is that ceramic tile starts to look more attractive than sheet vinyl; acrylic or cast-iron showers and tubs are better bets than fiberglass/gelcoat and porcelain steel.

Houses that are better insulated and more tightly sealed also put a premium on effective ventilation, not only to keep indoor air quality high but also to protect the building from an accumulation of moisture in wall and ceiling cavities. And, as the need for good ventilation has increased, so has the number of products that are available to consumers.

Bathrooms serve the same fundamental needs they always have. That's not going to change. But the nuts and bolts of how bathrooms are designed and built are different and will continue to evolve.

PLANNING

Smart bathroom design incorporates strategies

that save water and energy

YOUR

and includes features that allow

homeowners to age in place.

BATHROOM

Contemporary American bathrooms bear little resemblance to the small, plain spaces that many baby boomers grew up with. Just as houses—on average—have increased in size, so have most bathrooms. As a culture, we expect more than we used to: bigger, better, and more useful.

If you walked into a new master bath and found a sink, a toilet, and a 60-in. tub that doubled as a shower, it might seem slightly inadequate even if it had absolutely no functional shortcomings. It's not unusual now to find both a large soaking tub and a walk-in shower along with a double-sink vanity in a master bath. You'll find bathrooms with fireplaces, bathrooms with chandeliers, and bathrooms with upholstered furniture and heavy drapes. Surfaces might be tile, stone, or a man-made synthetic that looks just like stone. Not everyone has a budget to splurge on those kinds of luxuries, yet even when designs are more modest by necessity, there still is a broad range of plumbing fixtures and building materials to choose from.

Many of the decisions you'll make about bathroom design come from how the space will be used: Is it a powder room on the first floor used primarily by guests? A bath attached to an upstairs guest room? A child's bath? A master bath? A bathroom that will be used by someone with diminished physical capabilities? These are all key questions because they guide the choice of materials, the allocation of space, and the selection of color, lighting, and other design elements.

It doesn't make much sense to choose delicate, water-sensitive materials for a bathroom to be used by young children. Give them a space where they can splash in the tub without worrying whether the floor gets wet. Conversely, there aren't many youngsters who would send up a red flag when the vanity countertop is plastic laminate rather than Italian marble.

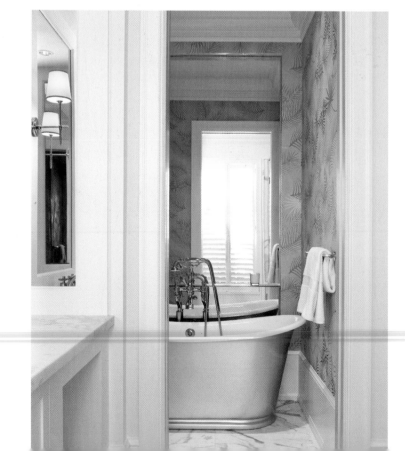

facing page top · Wood paneling and trim details give this powder room a formal feel, but a large mirror prevents the dark colors from feeling confining.

facing page bottom · A large soaking tub in its own nook can be the centerpiece of a master bath when a splurge on materials and square footage is in the budget.

above · When space allows, a custom shower and separate tub make a complete bathroom. This one gets extra light from a bank of windows set high enough in the wall to preserve privacy.

In a master bath, on the other hand, design choices get a little more complicated. Aesthetics equal—or may even overtake—the practical. For someone with a lot of work and family responsibilities, a long soak in a comfortable bathtub can be a restorative escape from routine.

Whether you'll be working through new construction or a renovation, a good place to start is by making basic choices on how the bathroom will be used, how much space it needs, and generally what kinds of fixtures and materials are most appropriate for its intended purpose. Unless the construction budget is unlimited (a rarity these days), the answers to those questions will have a lot to do with a successful design.

above • The wide band of river rock makes an attractive and functional detail behind the sink. It is repeated in the shower for cohesiveness in the room.

Expect the Unexpected when Remodeling

Remodeling any room is something of a guessing game because you never really know what you're going to find until you dive in. Bathrooms take that basic fact of life and up the ante; you're more likely to find hidden problems here than in almost any other part of the house simply because there's so much potential for water damage.

Be prepared to do more demolition than you expected or wanted. That means you need to build in an allowance for higher labor and materials costs as well as plan for the possibility of an extended construction schedule. It would be a rare remodel where the contractor doesn't approach you at least once with an unexpected issue. Problems can be solved—just don't be surprised when they pop up.

right • Careful materials selection makes all the difference in this bathroom. The ribbon-striped wood in the vanity and mirror plays well with the white tile, and nothing overwhelms the eye.

The success of this bath is the limited number of colors that work together. Pale green tile gives this bathroom a soft iridescence, while the black tile border complements the vanity base.

Putting Ideas into Practice

One early decision is the extent to which you will involve professional planners in designing a new bathroom. There is no right answer, but bigger budgets and bigger bathrooms make a more compelling case for hiring a pro than does a limited remodel involving mostly cosmetic upgrades.

Bathroom renovations in older houses often involve knocking down walls to make more room. A good contractor will be able to tell whether the walls you want to remove bear any structural loads or are simply partitions that can be yanked out without worrying whether the ceiling will collapse. But a designer or architect will be able to help you see design possibilities that even a good builder might miss; it's just a question of training and emphasis.

Even if you hire a designer, you should be willing to bring more to the table than yes or no answers to his or her suggestions. Educate yourself about the architectural style of your house to get a feel for what kind of renovation will work best. Start a clip file of magazine articles that show bathrooms you like, and start collecting information on fans, toilets, showerheads, countertops, tile, and anything else you'll need to make a decision about.

Stuffing clips into file folders works just fine, although software such as Evernote (a free download) makes it even easier to save text, photos, or Web pages to a laptop and smart phone. The information can be called up quickly if you need to explain something to a builder or designer, or when you're shopping for paint, lights, or cabinet pulls.

Regardless of the kind of pro you hire, do your homework so you go into the project understanding basically what's involved. There are many resources that can help, and one of them is the National Kitchen & Bath Association, which offers a free workbook to help you organize your ideas and give you some design and layout basics. In addition, visit a local kitchen and bath showroom to get a look at what's available.

Should You Be Your Own General Contractor?

Most homeowners don't have the skills to renovate a bathroom themselves, but it may be tempting to act as your own general contractor. That means you'd find and hire your own subcontractors rather than rely on a contractor to do it for you. Unless you're unusually well connected and have above average technical knowledge, this isn't a good idea.

Although it costs more to work through a general contractor, you're getting the benefit of his or her experience, access to skilled subcontractors, and knowledgeable oversight on the site. Plus, you have a better chance of getting the job done on schedule. For a strictly cosmetic overhaul you may not need a general contractor. Laying tile, painting, and minor plumbing are all possible for motivated (and skilled) homeowners looking to save some money and enjoy the process. You can hire a plumber or electrician for those jobs you know you're not qualified to do. But when the job is anything more than minor, bring in a professional.

facing page top • A large stone vanity top with an undermount sink and an open base provides plenty of storage without seeming visually overwhelming. A glass shower surround helps to keep the room light and airy.

above left • Wallpaper adds an attractive splash of color, especially when paired with a white tub and a light-colored floor.

left • Louvered shutters are one way of adding light and ventilation to a bathroom while preserving privacy.

Getting the Most from a Tiny Space

The challenge in designing small bathrooms is finding ways to make these rooms seem larger than they really are while incorporating features the owners want.

In this Bellevue, Washington, bath, which measures less than 56 sq. ft. overall, designer Debbi Cleary used light from a skylight and glass-block panels near the tub to enhance a sense of volume and openness. The glass block ensures privacy while admitting a lot of light, and it has the additional advantage of diffusing light—the neighbor's rust-color roof became a swirl of warm color, creating what Cleary calls "a soft intimacy."

Frameless glass walls around the extra deep, 3-ft. by 5-ft. soaking tub allow it to double as a shower while letting natural light flood the rest of the room.

Using a low-key, light color palette is one strategy to help small spaces feel larger. Here, a simple range of colors and materials unites the vanity with the shower so that the space flows smoothly.

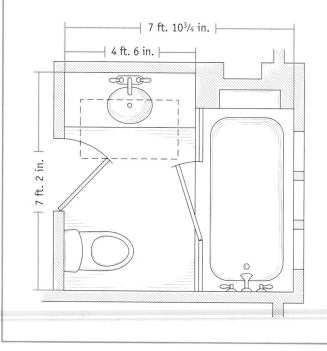

far left • Natural light is abundant in this small bathroom thanks to a wall of glass block, frameless glass panels around the tub, and an overhead skylight.

left • A fixture over the vanity directs light both up and down, enhancing the volume of the room.

below • The glass-block panels admit light without sacrificing privacy. The diffused patterns of light reflecting off a rust-colored roof nearby are a bonus.

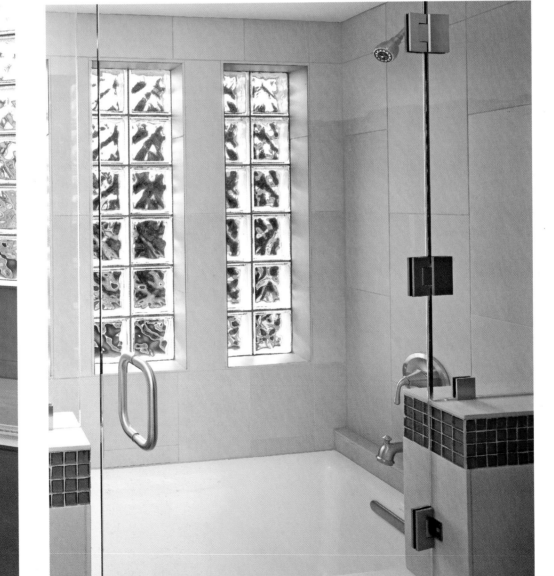

Hiring the Right People

If you've decided to hire someone to renovate your bathroom, you might choose a designer (or architect) plus a contractor or look for a builder who's been trained in design as well as construction; these pros are often part of a firm called design/build. Some pros have degrees in architecture but have chosen to stay on the construction side of the business, making for a valuable combination of skills.

ARCHITECTS

- Architects are the most highly trained and able to handle the widest variety of renovation problems, including structural repairs and alterations.

- Architects may charge a percentage of the overall project budget or by the hour.

- An architect may simply provide construction drawings or actually oversee the work as well.

- If the scope of the renovation seems to call for an architect, talk to several and choose one whose work you like and who seems to understand your budget and your objectives.

BUILDING CONTRACTORS/GENERAL CONTRACTORS

- General contractors (GCs) hire subcontractors for specific parts of the job while retaining overall responsibility for the work and scheduling.

- Meet with several prospective GCs and building contractors, not just the one recommended by your neighbor or brother-in-law. Ask to see a portfolio of their work. Ask for references and take the time to make those calls.

- When you find a contractor you like, ask to see proof of liability insurance, get his or her license number and check that it's valid, and request any other documentation that may be required of contractors in your community.

- Do not start work without a signed contract that spells out the scope of the work, when payments are to be made, and how change orders should be handled.

DESIGNERS

- Hiring a professional designer might be a good idea if the remodel requires extensive cosmetic changes, even moving walls, but doesn't affect the basic structure or appearance of the house.

- Find a designer who has been certified by the National Kitchen & Bath Association. There are several levels of certification: associate, certified, and certified master designer (CMKBD). The last requires the most training, but designers at all levels must pass written exams and have formal design education.

- Designers will be able to offer advice for all phases of the renovation.

- Interior decorators (not the same thing as a designer) have different training and specialize in furnishings, paint, color, and other surface decorations.

- As with contractors, ask for references and portfolios.

above · The simple glass splash guard helps to keep water in check in this curbless shower, particularly since the showerhead is centered in the space.

left · A full-width glass panel adds contemporary flair to this traditional-styled bath.

Whether you're remodeling or building new, keeping a few basic design principles in mind can be helpful. Every family's needs and every house are a little different, so rather than simply copying a floor plan you've seen elsewhere and hoping it will work in your house, make use of design fundamentals to help you develop a floor plan that will work for you.

Some of these design strategies are based on ideas found in the book *A Pattern Language*, by Christopher Alexander.

- Avoid layouts with more than one access door.

- Create an entrance alcove for a bathroom off a hallway to provide an added measure of privacy.

- A well-shaped bathroom is a square or a rectangle whose length is not more than twice its width.

- Good bathrooms have a clear central area where you can wash off or dry off. Fixtures like the tub and toilet should be located in alcoves at the edges of the room.

- Natural light is important. If the room can have only one window, locate it so it illuminates what you see when you first enter the room.

- Use the "intimacy gradient" in designing a floor plan by locating the most private parts of the bathroom farthest from the door.

- If space permits, pair a master bath and a dressing room. Custom cabinets can combine open shelves, drawers, and hanging space that best suit individual needs. Some manufacturers also offer cabinetry that would be ideal for a dressing room or walk-in closet with features such as a pull-out ironing board and a pull-up door that hides a clothes iron and other supplies.

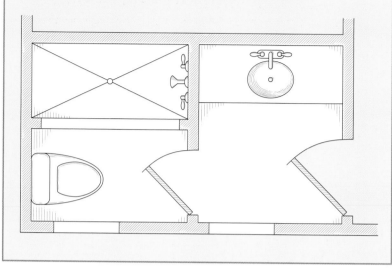

The Intimacy Gradient Applied to Bathrooms

The most intimate sections of a bathroom should be farthest from the door. In a small bath, use compartments with doors.

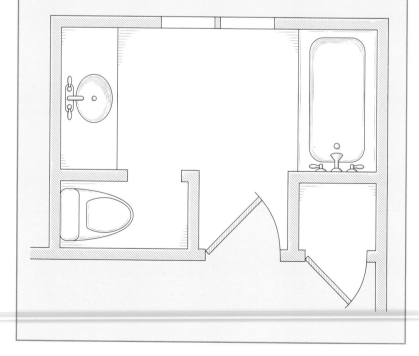

An Entry Transition and a Central Space Improve a Bathroom

Separate alcoves for different functions give a bathroom a roomlike quality. A small transition space changes the feel of the room.

Create a Dressing Room

Consider all kinds of storage needs in the early stages of your new bathroom design. If space and budget allow, create an alcove or new room adjacent to the bathroom for use as a walk-in dressing room. Open and closed shelves as well as drawers and rods of various sizes will make the space most efficient.

above • A dressing area next to the bath borrows some light via a transom high on the bathroom wall. Two-tiered hanging bars save space.

left • Renovations sometime permit bathroom expansions into an unused closet or utility room. A walk-in closet with both open shelves and drawers offers plenty of storage.

Making Design Accessible

Although the principles of universal design have been slow to trickle into residential design, you can incorporate accessibility into a bathroom whether remodeling or building new. Universal design principles can make a house more comfortable for anyone living there, not just someone using a cane or wheelchair or dealing with the infirmities of old age.

Because bathrooms are used so frequently and for such a variety of daily tasks, they are among the most important spaces at home to design this way.

Universal design makes it easier for those who have been disabled or injured to take care of themselves. It also is a way of making bathrooms adaptable to people as they get older and gradually become less capable physically, even to the point of helping the bathroom accommodate the homeowner plus a caregiver. Some bathroom features can be built so they are convertible as needs change: a vanity whose top can be lowered simply and quickly for someone in a wheelchair, for example. But some features must be incorporated into the room when it's built.

A shower without a threshold makes access easier for someone using a wheelchair, and a handheld shower simplifies bathing.

above · This shower stall is ideal for children as well as those who need to sit while bathing, thanks to the lower-than-normal niche for toiletries plus the shower controls and handheld sprayer being located in the center of the wall.

left · A bathroom without visual barriers seems open and inviting, even when the space is relatively small.

Lessons in Designs That Accommodate Changes in Life

Thirty years ago, Cindy Leibrock was a disenchanted interior designer, finding fewer spiritual rewards in "making rich people look richer." Eventually she found a new calling with universal design. Later, Leibrock and her husband built a new house in Livermore, Colorado, that melded universal design with the principles of sustainable building.

After finishing up the house, her husband slipped on the racquetball court, rupturing an Achilles tendon, and Leibrock went in for a hip replacement. Virtually overnight, they faced circumstances that normally would be life changing. Her doctor suggested they check into a nursing home until they were well enough to maneuver around their own home, but their forethought in incorporating universal design into their plans made that unnecessary. They recuperated at home.

Injured in a freak bicycle accident in 1998, universal design specialist Rosemarie Rossetti suddenly found herself living in a house that made daily life a trial. The second floor and basement of her two-story home were inaccessible and while modifications helped, they were inadequate. In the end, she and her husband Mark began building a house they hope will be a national model for accessible design as well as their home, called the Universal Design Living Laboratory.

To both Leibrock and Rossetti, universal design is not about an after-the-fact adaptation to disability; it is about planning for its inevitability in a way that makes any home more appealing.

ALLOW ENOUGH ROOM

Wheelchairs and walkers need extra maneuvering room, so one of the first objectives should be to make doorways, showers, and floor plans generous enough to handle them.

The Center for Universal Design at North Carolina State University has developed a number of useful recommendations and sample floor plans for bathrooms, many of which are available for free online.

Some of the layout basics include the following:

- Make doorways 36 in. wide, with no threshold.
- Provide a 60-in.-diameter turning space and 30-in. by 48-in. clear floor space at each fixture (clear spaces can overlap each other).
- Make a 36-in. clear space in front of and to one side of the toilet.
- Make lavatory countertops at least 32 in. high with a 29-in.-high knee space. It's fine to make the knee hole accessible with removable panels or folding doors, but hot-water lines should be covered to prevent burns.
- The shower should be a minimum of 3 ft. by 5 ft.
- Leave a minimum clear zone of 1 ft. 6 in. between the edge of the counter and the door opening.
- Make sure the shower is equipped with an antiscald mixing valve or a programmable control that allows the bather to set the temperature accurately before venturing into the shower.
- Position tub and shower controls so they are within easy reach of someone in a wheelchair rather than centered over the tub. The same goes for electrical outlets and switches.
- Consider a handheld shower that can be reached from a seated position, which is easier for someone in a wheelchair to use.
- Install a toilet that is compliant with the Americans with Disabilities Act (ADA). It will have a seat height of between 15 in. and 19 in., a good "transfer height" for someone in a wheelchair.

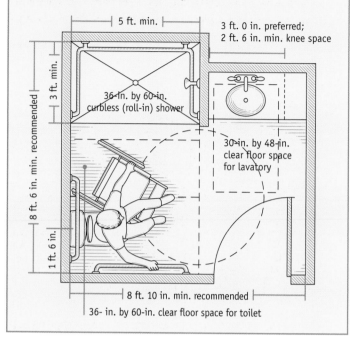

A Layout that Allows Room for Maneuvering

Reinforcing for grab bars must be provided.

5 ft. min.

3 ft. 0 in. preferred; 2 ft. 6 in. min. knee space

3 ft. min.

36-in. by 60-in. curbless (roll-in) shower

8 ft. 6 in. min. recommended

30-in. by 48-in. clear floor space for lavatory

1 ft. 6 in.

8 ft. 10 in. min. recommended

36- in. by 60-in. clear floor space for toilet

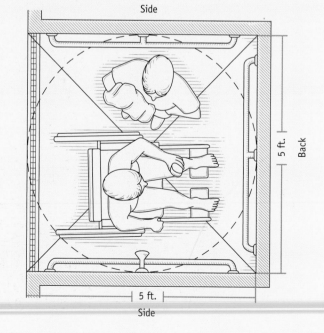

Larger Showers for Assistance with Bathing

A 5-ft. by 5-ft. curbless shower provides space so an attendant can assist with bathing and allows a wheelchair user to turn around within the shower.

Side

5 ft.

Back

5 ft.

Side

Making a Bathroom Safe and Convenient

When thinking about accessibility, it's important to think ahead and think broadly. The bathroom here was designed for someone in a wheelchair, but it could just as easily be found in the home of people without disabilities.

right • Providing lots of room around the toilet, along with a handheld shower installed at a comfortable height, makes bathing much easier.

left and below • In this bathroom designed by Universal Design specialist Cindy Leibrock, conventional barriers have been eliminated. The front panel in the vanity can be removed, allowing someone in a wheelchair to use the sink. Any exposed hot-water lines should be covered to prevent burns.

REMOVE OBSTRUCTIONS

Door thresholds make navigating a wheelchair difficult. In fact, any abrupt change in floor height is an impediment to a wheelchair and a potential trip hazard for someone with reduced motor skills. Remove rugs from the room as well (unless they can be installed so the edges are flush with the rest of the floor).

If a threshold is a mere inconvenience, the curb on a conventional shower is a virtual roadblock. Curbless showers are designed without a lip at the entrance so a wheelchair can roll right in. Sloping the floor toward the drain keeps the water where it belongs.

above • **Although narrow, this bathroom has a curbless shower with a handheld shower, plus a vanity area with an open space below for easy access.**

The Practicalities of a Curbless Shower

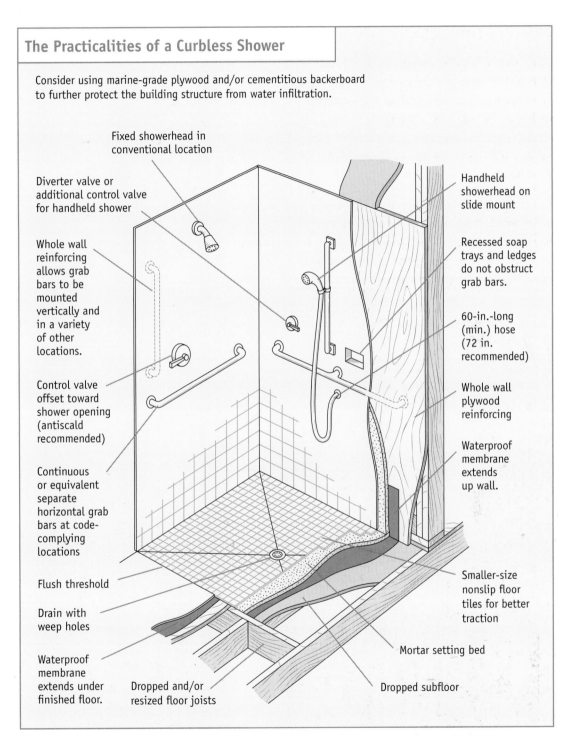

Consider using marine-grade plywood and/or cementitious backerboard to further protect the building structure from water infiltration.

Fixed showerhead in conventional location

Diverter valve or additional control valve for handheld shower

Whole wall reinforcing allows grab bars to be mounted vertically and in a variety of other locations.

Control valve offset toward shower opening (antiscald recommended)

Continuous or equivalent separate horizontal grab bars at code-complying locations

Flush threshold

Drain with weep holes

Waterproof membrane extends under finished floor.

Dropped and/or resized floor joists

Handheld showerhead on slide mount

Recessed soap trays and ledges do not obstruct grab bars.

60-in.-long (min.) hose (72 in. recommended)

Whole wall plywood reinforcing

Waterproof membrane extends up wall.

Smaller-size nonslip floor tiles for better traction

Mortar setting bed

Dropped subfloor

left · A pedestal sink is more convenient than a standard vanity for someone in a wheelchair. A better option, though, is a vanity with a completely open face.

INSTALL GRAB BARS

Grab bars provide welcome stability for someone whose balance is a little off, someone recovering from an injury, or a child who may need an extra handhold. The time to start thinking about them is before any finished walls go in. Grab bars and anything that might temporarily serve as a grab bar—including towel racks and toilet paper holders—must be solidly anchored to wall framing.

Solid blocking between studs should be provided at heights where these accessories will be mounted. An even better approach is to install a continuous layer of ¾-in. plywood beneath the drywall, allowing solid points of attachment wherever they are needed in the future.

In keeping with her effort to keep designs flexible, universal design specialist Cindy Leibrock (see the sidebar on p. 21) installed a pair of removable grab bars flanking the toilet in her bathroom (see the photos on the facing page). They can be installed in a few minutes, without tools, by popping off two wall tiles. When the bars aren't needed, they can be removed and the tiles put back in place. The conversion is fast and easy.

In addition to the more conventional horizontal type, consider vertical grab bars near the toilet and in the shower. They're especially handy for men folk trying to use the facilities.

An overhead track and sling can be used to move a person from the toilet to the tub. When the sling isn't needed, it can easily be slipped off the end of the track and put away.

If you're planning on staying in your home and want some help making alterations that will make it easier, consider contacting a Certified Aging-in-Place Specialist, or CAP, through the National Association of Home Builders (www.nahb.org/aginginplace).

above • Double-wide doors and the lack of a threshold are good start toward making this bathroom accessible for a wheelchair. The high tub and conventional vanity, however, are drawbacks.

left • This ceiling-mounted sling can take someone from tub to toilet. When not in use, the sling can be removed from the track and stowed away.

above • An assist when you need it: A sturdy rail can be attached to a wall-mounted plate in seconds. When not in use, the rail pivots up and out of the way. It can be removed entirely, with the mounting plate concealed by a tile.

Handicapped-Accessible with an Old-Fashioned Feel

The master bath in this oceanfront house in Cape Elizabeth, Maine, was part of a ground-up rebuild guided by strict property and water setbacks as well as limits on how much of the property could be covered with impervious materials. The owner, a single woman with an extended family, wanted the bath to be handicapped-accessible and to have a tub with a view of the ocean.

With those parameters in mind, this narrow bath was designed to make every inch count.

The vanity is centered on one wall, with the soaking tub on the ocean side of the room and the handicapped-accessible shower on the other. Access to the master bedroom is via a pocket door that will rarely be closed.

"The owner came with antique family furnishings and a strong idea that the décor of the house should be neutral in color and filled with natural light, to show off views of the ocean and sky from every room," says architect John Whipple. Those design goals are reflected in the new bathroom, with large windows at one end for light and views, recycled southern pine flooring near the tub, and an antique framed mirror over the vanity.

At the opposite end of the room, the floor and shower surround are finished in marble. The floor of the easy-access shower is pebbled, providing good traction as well as an interesting color and texture contrast.

Although the color choices at first seemed overly neutral, they've created a room that feels summery and bright regardless of the time of year.

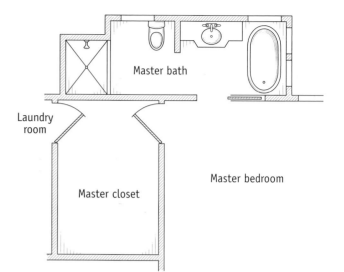

Master bath

Laundry room

Master closet

Master bedroom

right • While pine flooring dominates one end of the room, the other is finished in marble. The color palette is simple and understated.

above • With a mainly white-and-black backdrop, the wood mirror frame is a detail that stands out clearly.

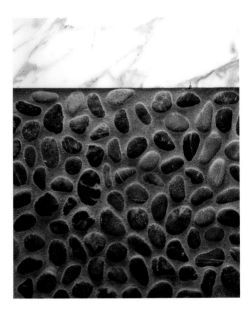

above • The floor in the shower area is marble while the shower floor itself is small river rock for an appealing color contrast and good traction when wet.

above • A new master bath in this Maine oceanfront house includes a large tub with stunning water views. Recycled pine flooring helps to give the bath an old-fashioned flavor.

Managing Energy and Water Costs

A key principle of green building is resource conservation, which boils down to reducing waste and inefficiencies wherever possible. Even if you have no interest in building a home that will be eligible for certification under one of several green building programs, water conservation inevitably leads to energy conservation. Both are attractive.

Saving water does not have to mean either discomfort or added costs. Houses designed for efficient water use can be easier and more comfortable to live in, as well as less expensive to operate.

There are two basic strategies for using less water: choosing toilets, faucets, and showerheads that use less (for more on this, see Chapters 2 and 3), and making basic design choices in your plumbing system to minimize waste.

For the most part, a smart plumbing design is something built into the house, not something that's easy to do later unless floors and ceilings are removed--not your average weekend do-it-yourself (DIY) project. But new construction presents many opportunities, such as opting for a "home run" distribution system over a more conventional trunk-and-branch layout for supply lines. Running a separate supply line to each fixture or outlet minimizes heat loss, speeds delivery of hot water, and consequently means less waste.

Another systems approach is a hot-water circulation system, which can be plumbed into an existing bathroom as well as built into a new one at a relatively low cost. This system eliminates the wait for hot water at shower and sink.

When privacy isn't an issue, large windows in the shower let in a great deal of light and make it seem as if you're showering outdoors.

In addition to saving water, good plumbing design also saves energy. Something as simple as insulating hot-water lines between the water heater and each point of use will make a difference. More complex strategies, such as a drain-water heat recovery, cost more initially but also can reduce hot-water costs substantially.

Reusing gray water (what goes down the drain after a shower or from a washing machine) also holds promise for using less water. While gray water isn't potable, it's not especially dirty either, and it can be used for watering the lawn or garden or for flushing toilets—providing that local plumbing codes allow it and your plumber knows how to set it up.

All of these things are worth discussing with your plumber when you're building new or undertaking a major bathroom remodel. You'll find that taking relatively simple steps while the house is under construction may pay dividends down the road.

A full-length vanity top with two integrated sinks is a great feature in a busy bathroom. Pull-out steps make it easier for children to wash up and brush their teeth.

FIXTURES

Fixtures are the workhorses of the bathroom, but they can

add style as well as functionality. Even the humble toilet can make

an aesthetic contribution to the room.

Sinks

A perfectly serviceable bathroom sink made from vitreous china can be had at any home center for about $50, maybe less. It will be plain in design and white in color, and it will likely last for many years. However, if your tastes wander toward the more exotic, there is no shortage of options. Like tubs, toilets, and other bathroom fixtures, sinks now run the stylistic gamut in a corresponding wide array of materials.

In addition to cost, there are three other considerations: how the sink is installed, what it's made from, and what kind of aesthetic role it's destined to play in overall bathroom design.

There are five basic sink configurations: those that drop into the top of the vanity (called self-rimming), those that are mounted from below, freestanding consoles or pedestals, wall-mounted sinks, and sinks that sit on top of the counter, usually called "vessel" sinks, a trademark of the Kohler Co., but made by many other companies.

The material a sink is manufactured from does make a difference, but not a lot. There are, practically speaking, no functional differences between a $2,000 hammered copper basin and the $50 lavatory from your local home center. Basic vitreous china is durable and easy to keep clean, and for those reasons is a good choice. But metal, stone, wood, glass, and solid-surface sinks are alternatives. Some are harder to maintain than others, and most are more expensive than a simple china drop-in.

A bathroom sink can be a centerpiece of the room's design or simply a basin for washing and brushing your teeth. Deciding what you want the sink to do is a good first step.

This large console sink offers more countertop storage for toiletries than a pedestal sink, and its shaped legs complement an old-fashioned décor.

above left · A vessel sink with a matching tile backsplash and wall-mounted faucets complements a house built in the Southwestern style.

above right · There's no rule that says a sink has to be white. This undermount commands attention even though its unobtrusive.

left · A counter and sink formed as a single component are attractively contemporary and much easier to keep clean than a conventional drop-in sink.

SELF-RIMMING SINKS

The most basic design is a self-rimming sink that drops into a recess in the top of the vanity. These sinks are compatible with any countertop material, a plus; but they also are harder to keep clean because the seam where the sink joins the counter inevitably collects grime, potentially a big minus.

One exception to this rule is a drop-in set in a tile countertop. The sink can be adjusted in height relative to the substrate so that when tile is brought up to the perimeter the surfaces are flush. When the seam is caulked, there's no place for grunge to collect.

While the self-rimming design is an old standby, there are many examples of beautifully finished self-rimming sinks that are anything but basic. Some companies have in-house artists who paint designs by hand before the sinks are fired. And designs can be customized to suit a particular color scheme or room theme: seashells or mermaids at a beach cottage, for instance, or flowers for an avid gardener. Finishes incorporating metallic or other special paints and glazes aren't necessarily as robust as a basic vitreous china surface, though, so handle and clean accordingly.

From an installation standpoint, self-rimming sinks are among the most forgiving, something to consider if you're doing the work yourself and don't have a lot of experience. A template supplied with the sink gives the exact shape of the cutout, and as long as the hole is reasonably close to the size of the sink, the sink will fit just fine.

The scalloped edges of this sink are an attractive detail, especially when set against a dark countertop.

left • Self-rimming sinks are set in a cutout in the vanity top. Although they typically are economical, they can potentially leak around the rim.

below left • While oval self-rimming sinks are commonplace, there are other shapes to choose from, like this flowerlike sink.

below • This simple self-rimming sink is a solid low-cost choice for a child's bath, where aesthetic expectations are probably a bit relaxed.

PEDESTALS AND CONSOLES

Pedestal sinks take up very little floor area, and they're also easy to clean because they're typically cast as a single unit without joints or seams.

A small pedestal sink is ideal for a powder room, where it's used mostly for hand washing. But unless it's unusually large, a pedestal sink is not such a great choice in a busy, everyday bathroom. Without a countertop or any undercounter storage, there's very little room for a hairbrush, toothbrush, hair dryers, and all the other things that find their way into the bathroom. Extra storage in the form of a medicine cabinet or cupboard will have to be provided. Even then, where do you park the shaving cream in the morning?

Console sinks are a variation on the theme, with legs made of metal or china supporting the basin instead of a single pedestal. A towel rack can be worked into the frame, giving consoles a slight edge over pedestals in convenience, and some consoles come with fairly large surfaces around the sink. Smaller models have the same advantages and drawbacks as a pedestal design: easier to clean than some other sink types, perhaps, but lacking storage.

In addition to being one-piece china fixtures, consoles can combine other materials—a wood or stone counter surface with a self-rimming or undermount sink, for example.

Placing two pedestal sinks next to each other is an alternative to the double-bowl vanity that has become so common.

above • Pedestal sinks take up very little floor space, and when paired with nearby storage, their small surrounds aren't much of a drawback.

above right • Exposed bracing on the frame of this sleek, contemporary console can be used for a wash cloth or hand towel.

right • Although console sinks often evoke an old-time architectural style, they also can be contemporary in shape and color.

UNDERMOUNTS

Undermounts are attached to the bottom of the counter surface with metal clips and sealed with caulk. When installed correctly, there's virtually no chance of a leak at the rim, and the vanity top is a breeze to clean because there's no sink rim to get in the way. From a design point of view, undermounts are understated and unobtrusive.

They're ideal for many countertop choices—stone, concrete, and other monolithic surfaces—and not so good for others. It's no doubt possible to mount one to a laminate counter, but not without a good deal of effort. So if you're going with laminate, better to pick another style.

Solid-surface undermounts can be glued directly to the counter for a completely seamless installation with no chance of collecting grime between sink and counter. That's a plus in the kitchen and works to the same advantage in the bathroom, as long as you like the material. One-piece sink countertops also are available at home centers.

above • Sinks don't have to be of a single color. Manufactured and hand-painted designs are widely available in a variety of custom and stock designs.

right • Undermount sinks in a plain color let the texture and color of the countertop dominate.

facing page left • Paired with a graceful single-stem faucet, this rectangular undermount looks clean and contemporary.

facing page right • Undermount sinks are a modern adaptation, but period faucets, a marble vanity top, and the demilune vanity give this bathroom old-school charm.

WALL-MOUNTED SINKS

Wall-mounted sinks have the same pros and cons as pedestals, with one obvious difference. Because there's nothing touching the floor, cleaning is much simpler. Wall-mounts also share the same disadvantage, namely a lack of storage for cosmetics and toiletries. They make the most sense in a guest bath or powder room where they're not taking the full brunt of daily use.

Large, old-fashioned wall-mounts lend a great flavor to a period home or farmhouse, but they also are available in a number of more contemporary styles. They range from sinks suited for a corner installation to those with the faucet mount on the side to cut their intrusion into the room to a bare minimum. Some even come with a shelf below the bowl for storing hand towels or soap.

above • **This contemporary wall-hung sink takes up very little room, and it offers just enough of a countertop for a powder room.**

far left • This is what wall-hung sinks used to look like, and the sturdy, no-nonsense style can still be successful.

left • A wall-mounted sink offers no obstacles to cleaning the floor, but like a small pedestal sink, it doesn't offer much room for storing toiletries.

below • Small and colorful, this wall-mounted sink would be ideal in a powder room.

ABOVE-COUNTER SINKS

The trendy above-counter sink is a stylistic throwback to an age when indoor plumbing amounted to a basin atop a bureau or side table, in other words pre-modern plumbing. But there's nothing outdated about the look now.

Above-counter sinks are available in glass, stone, bronze, and vitreous china, as well as a range of prices, so they should be able to fit most design schemes and budgets. They can be paired with surface-mounted faucets (make sure the neck of the faucet is tall enough) or faucets that pop directly out of the wall.

There are a couple of practical things to keep in mind if you're leaning in this direction. First and foremost, you'll need to do more advance planning. Above-counter sinks come in many heights, and you'll need those specs to set the counter height of the vanity. And if you want in-the-wall plumbing, it will take careful coordination with your builder or plumbing contractor. He'll need the exact location of the sink before roughing in supply lines and drains.

above • Above-counter sinks are reminiscent of the washbasins widely used in days before indoor plumbing.

top • Because wall-mounted faucets don't sit on the countertop, there is more decking available for toiletries. However, these kinds of faucets require early conversations with your plumber or builder to ensure their placement can be accommodated.

above • Above-counter sinks are available in a variety of shapes, colors, styles, and materials and can be paired with contemporary or period decors.

Because all of the sink is above
countertop height, vanity
height may have to be adjusted.

Countertops

The green building boom has added considerably to the repertoire of bathroom countertop options. Old favorites include tile, stone and stone composites, solid surface, plastic laminate, concrete, and wood. To that, you may now add a variety of countertops made from recycled materials, such as glass and paper.

No matter what the material, the choice still boils down to a few issues: durability, how much maintenance the surface requires, price, and compatibility with other features in the room. And the right balance of features varies depending on where the counter gets installed. In a bathroom used mainly by children, you'd be wise to pick something that cleans up easily, wears well, and doesn't cost too much. Plastic laminate or solid surface are two good options. In a high-budget master bathroom where materials are carefully orchestrated, it's unlikely plastic laminate would be your first choice, despite its many practical advantages. A powder room used mostly by guests is a good place to splurge on a countertop with lots of visual appeal: a special piece of stone or a striking piece of highly figured wood. You're not installing much of it, so the cost per square foot isn't an overwhelming factor. You can afford to make a good impression on your visitors.

In addition to the price of materials, there is the labor of fabrication and installation. Some counters (wood, plastic laminate, and recycled paper) can be cut and shaped on-site. That can result in some dollar and time savings over such materials as stone, recycled glass, and concrete, all of which must be fabricated with special equipment in a shop off-site (and which also can be cut incorrectly). With this in mind, be sure to do your research on fabricators and installers.

top · Wood countertops, while not as common as stone, solid surface, or laminate, make excellent vanity tops, providing they are finished carefully and the finish is maintained.

above · Stone and manufactured stone, which is mostly quartz, make durable, attractive countertops and are available in many colors and patterns.

far left • Countertops can be integrated with the backsplash to make a pleasing whole. Here, mosaic tile is an interesting counterpoint to a monolithic vanity top.

left • Because stone is available in long blanks, it can be manufactured into a seamless countertop even on a double-vanity. Undermount sinks give the installation a crisp, contemporary look.

below • A dark, textured countertop complements the cherry vanity.

The list of green materials being used to fabricate countertops is surprisingly long. "Green" means the material helps to save energy or natural resources (or both), that it has no ill effects on health, and that in mining, manufacturing, or harvesting it there is a minimal impact on the environment. If you're building a house to the standards of Leadership in Energy and Environmental Design (LEED), selecting countertops with high recycled content wins you points that count toward certification. But the truth is, many of these newer materials are just plain interesting as well as attractive.

IceStone^{SM}, BioGlass^{SM}, EnviroSLAB^{TM}, Vetrazzo$^®$, and several other companies, for example, make counters out of recycled glass in a good selection of snazzy colors. PaperStone$^®$ and Eco-Top^{TM} countertops are made from recycled paper, and a company called Alkemi combines aluminum scrap and polyester resin to make a really striking countertop. Craft-Art makes counters in end-grain bamboo. The revival of linoleum, which is slowly reemerging from the shadow of sheet vinyl, means more suppliers and installers. All of these materials may be attractive whether you're trying to be environmentally conscious or just looking for something unique.

Concrete is another option that has steadily gained ground in the bathroom as well as the kitchen. Because of its growing popularity, there are more fabricators than even a few years ago. Concrete can be cast into virtually any shape and enlivened with embedded objects and dyes for a highly custom look. If you go this route, make sure you get a seasoned fabricator and ask to see samples of his or her work; there is a learning curve in working with this material.

Stone is an excellent countertop material, but most types of stone should be sealed to prevent stains.

top · Concrete makes a very durable countertop, but like stone, it must be sealed to keep out water and stains.

above · Keeping a vanity top in the same color group as the rest of the room helps unify the space. Here, a low-key vanity top lets the profiles of the vanity face stand out.

Countertop Materials

LAMINATE
$

- Excellent choice for a child's bath.
- Enormous variety of colors and patterns available, including realistic wood and stone.
- One of the lowest-cost options available.
- Nonporous, easy to clean, and waterproof.
- Not suitable for undermount sinks because of exposed edges at sink opening.
- Need to maintain caulk around edges to protect substrate from water.

WOOD
$-$$

- Great variety in wood tones and figure.
- Can be fabricated with ordinary carpentry tools, making customizing simple.
- Some wood species are naturally resistant to moisture damage, but maintaining the finish is key to avoiding water spots or worse.
- Can be used with any sink type.
- If you want to go the green route, specify wood certified by the Forest Stewardship Council.

TILE
$-$$

- Ample variety in sizes and colors to fit just about any design theme.
- Easy to customize by mixing different colors and sizes of tile.
- Ceramic tile is nonporous and nonstaining but grout isn't, so it will need to be sealed
- Can be integrated with a tile backsplash.
- Surface is tough on glassware and other breakables.
- Damaged tiles can be removed and replaced (just remember to order a few extra and tuck them away).

RECYCLED-CONTENT MATERIALS
$-$$$

- Visually interesting and available in a wide range of colors.
- Recycled content is helpful when seeking green certification.
- Recycled glass counters with cement binders should be sealed to avoid stains.
- Some types of glass counters must be fabricated with specialized equipment.

SOLID SURFACE
$$

- Plenty of patterns and colors to choose from.
- Nonstaining, easy to maintain, and waterproof.
- Integral sink bowl an option for a seamless, easy-to-clean installation.
- Minor surface damage can be sanded out.
- Visually not as warm as wood, tile, and other nonplastic materials.

STONE COMPOSITES
$$

- Quartz and resin combinations are nonporous and impervious to water.
- Better stain resistance than natural stone and concrete.
- Many colors and patterns are available from several manufacturers.
- Fabricated like stone.
- Very hard and durable.

CONCRETE
$$-$$$

- Can be cast into any shape and easily customized.
- Can be treated with dyes and other surface treatments.
- Hard and durable.
- The number of local fabricators increasing.
- Surface can develop hairline cracks and will stain if not sealed.
- Thick concrete counters are heavy, so plan cabinetry accordingly.

NATURAL STONE
$$-$$$

- Lots of colors and patterns are available, and some kinds of stone are now sold in home-improvement centers, making it more affordable.
- Must be fabricated in specialized shops.
- Most natural stone should be sealed to keep out stains.
- Suitable for all sink types.

above · Choosing a countertop material that can be fabricated into long, unbroken spans eliminates seams, a cosmetic advantage.

above left · When the countertop is made from the same material as the wainscoting, different parts of the room blend together nicely. The color choice on the wall above the sink is an effective contrast with the light-colored marble.

left · An extra-thick counter gives this vanity mass. The heavy design of the wallpaper as well as the wood-edged mirror complement its weightiness.

Grand Lifestyle Meets Modern Realities

A 1920s stone house in the heart of Philadelphia had been built for a grand lifestyle, but the uninviting attic spaces, storage rooms, and closets on the third floor held little appeal for its contemporary owners.

Their plans were to rework this floor—what had been the servants' wing—to provide more family recreational space, and that meant opening up a cramped staircase and finding a new spot for the bathroom. Plans could not include disrupting either the stone façade of the house or its clay tile roof.

Space for the new bathroom was found in an existing T-shape closet located above the front entrance. The room came with a dormer and a casement window and did not require the addition of any dormers or bump-outs. The trick, however, was fitting a shower, toilet, sink, and storage space within the intersecting angles of the roof. Krieger + Associates Architects found enough room in one arm of the T for a shower stall and located the toilet in the other.

The shower enclosure is finished with 4¼-in.-square white tiles. The center of the room got heart pine floors, beadboard wainscoting, a marble vanity shelf, and a period-style pedestal sink. A custom radiator cover matches those in the rest of the house.

A narrow shelf next to the window serves as a vanity top. The custom radiator cover matches those in the rest of the house.

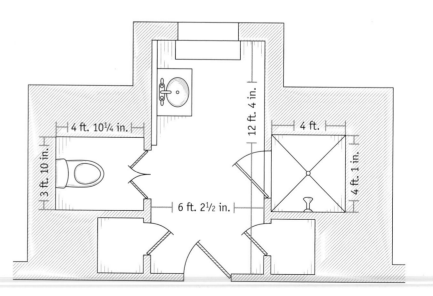

above · The central area of this small bathroom is flanked by two niches, one for a shower and another for a toilet. Heart pine flooring gives the room warmth.

above left · In the one arm of the room's T-shape layout, designers added the toilet, complete with a door for privacy.

left · A shower tucked into the other arm of a T-shape bathroom is finished in white tile to keep the space bright and appealing.

Faucets

To some extent, the choice of a faucet is dictated by the type of sink it will be partnered with. Pedestal or drop-in sinks typically come with holes along the back edge for mounting the faucet, and the distance between the holes determines the range of faucets that will fit. Above-counter sinks and undermounts often come without any holes, opening up more possibilities. Because there are so many variations in both sinks and faucets, it's a good idea to shop for them at the same time. You may find just the right faucet but not a sink that will accommodate it—better to learn that before the plumber arrives.

Among the most common types of faucets are centerset, widespread, wall-mounted, and monoblock (or single-hole) faucets.

Centersets have the spouts and one or two handles to control water flow on a shared base. They're compact, so they're well suited to small sinks and tight spaces.

Widespread faucets have individual control handles for hot and cold water and a separate one for the spout. They're for sinks with three holes on the back rim or for undermounts or above-counter sinks without holes when the faucet is mounted directly on the deck.

Wall-mounted faucets come with one or two control handles and are mounted directly behind or to the side of the sink. They're a little more complicated to install because all of the plumbing is buried in the wall, but they have the advantage of making it easier to clean around the sink.

In **monoblock** faucets, everything is housed in a single component. They require only a single hole in the sink or countertop.

above • Centerset faucets combine the faucets with a central spout. They can be very compact.

right • More contemporary in style, a monoblock incorporates the spout and control in a single unit.

above · Wall-mount faucets facilitate cleaning around the sink. Combined with an above-counter sink, they're very stylish, but make sure to plan ahead for in-wall plumbing.

above · Wall-mounted faucets come in a variety of contemporary styles.

above · In a widespread faucet, the faucets and spout are all separate pieces, better for larger sinks and counter installations.

Faucet finishes run the gamut from polished chrome or brass to brushed nickel and bronze. A process called physical vapor deposition (PVD) makes a more wear-resistant surface than conventional electroplating. The overall design of the bathroom, including fixture selection, walls, and countertop material, will help guide faucet selection. But in general, brushed or hammered surfaces don't show fingerprints and water spots as readily as polished chrome or brass.

It's entirely possible to spend a small fortune on a faucet for the sink, but at a certain point you're paying for aesthetics, not function. Cheap faucets are nothing but a headache, but it isn't necessary to break the bank to get a well-made faucet that will provide many years of trouble-free service. Look for all-metal construction, a PVD finish, and a valve design that doesn't use washers, such as a ceramic disc valve.

above · This monoblock faucet and sculptural wall-mounted sink make for a clean, uncluttered look.

above · When choosing a deck-mounted faucet for an above-counter sink, make sure its reach is enough to clear the lip of the sink.

right · With little room to spare in this guest bath, wall-mounted faucets are ideal. The frame-mounted sink and faucet combination is a contemporary departure from a more conventional pedestal sink.

Pairing a slab-like sink/vanity with a curving faucet is an attractive detail in this otherwise Spartan bath.

Faucets

The type of sink you choose helps dictate the type of faucet, but regardless of category, the range of finishes and styles for faucets is significant. Look for an all-metal design with a PVD finish.

4

1. A deck mounted monoblock faucet is sleek, contemporary, and a good match for an above-counter sink. 2. Wide-spread faucets are appropriate for sinks with three holes in the rim or for undermount sinks, where holes can be bored anywhere in the counter. 3. Period-style faucets are readily available in a variety of traditional finishes, such as polished chrome and nickel. 4. The contrast between a blocky, rectangular sink and a gooseneck faucet spout is interesting, and raising the height of the spout makes washing up a little more convenient. 5. Wall-mounted faucets eliminate clutter on the countertop or sink bib and facilitate cleaning.

Toilets

Toilets, the most fundamental of all bathroom fixtures, have undergone something of a revolution in the last few years. Beginning with a federal edict in 1995 that a toilet use no more than 1.6 gallons per flush (gpf), the industry has steadily ramped up performance with more efficient designs while lowering water consumption. The result is a wide selection of low-flow fixtures that actually work they way they're supposed to.

When building new or renovating, homeowners may be tempted to rely on the advice of only their plumbing contractor when it comes to what brand or model of toilet to install. But plumbers sometimes pick brands they're familiar with or buy through a supplier that only stocks toilets from certain manufacturers.

It can be tough to work up a lot of enthusiasm for choosing a toilet when glass tile, hand-painted sinks, and soaking tubs are beckoning. But given the number of times a toilet is used every day (Toto estimates that everyone in the house will flush five times), it makes more sense to knuckle down and do a little research.

BASIC VS. SPECIAL-ASSIST TOILETS

The basic toilet in America is a gravity-fed two-piece fixture made from vitreous china. It consists of a bowl that's bolted to the floor and a tank that's bolted to the bowl. It's assembled by the plumber on-site, and it uses the federally required 1.6 gpf.

This type of toilet is all that most of us need, but there are other types to choose from, including dual-flush, pressure-assist, and macerating toilets. These special-purpose toilets sometimes are a better choice, either from a functional or an aesthetic point of view (for more on these toilets, see pp. 62–63).

One-piece toilets are cast as a single piece of china. They tend to be less bulky and have a lower profile than conventional two-piece designs. But from a performance standpoint they don't work any better, and they are more expensive. They do have one advantage: they're easier to clean. With no seam between tank and bowl, there are fewer places for debris to collect.

top • What manufacturers call "comfort height" toilets were originally designed to meet requirements of the Americans with Disabilities Act.

above • In a basic two-piece toilet, castings clearly show the curved shapes of internal passageways, but in more contemporary designs, the outside of the base is smoothly contoured. A toilet like this is easier to clean.

Testing Performance

Manufacturers have solved design problems that plagued early low-flow toilets, and now consumers have a way of checking on performance before they buy. A testing protocol called Maximum Performance testing (MaP) checks performance, and results are readily available online. The program currently lists performance data for more than 1,400 toilets, and results are updated every four to six months.

Testers use soybean paste encased in a thin latex membrane in weights up to 1,000 grams to simulate real-world performance. Toilets are listed by manufacturer and model name, so it's easy to check on a fixture a plumber might be recommending. Toilets that meet federal WaterSense standards (1.28 gallons per flush) and ADA-compliant fixtures are also flagged.

To see the report, go to www.allianceforwaterefficiency.org.

top · Toilets sometimes don't look like toilets, as is the case with the iconic Kohler Hatbox®. Sleeker, unconventional designs are well suited to contemporary bathrooms.

above · Low-profile toilets have a contemporary look.

above · A one-piece toilet has fewer seams than a conventional two-piece design, making bathroom maintenance a little easier. Typically, however, this type of toilet is more expensive than the standard two-piece.

Special-Purpose Toilets

Sometimes a conventional two-piece toilet doesn't meet the needs of a particular family or installation. There are a number of options.

Pressure-Assist Toilets

That alarming whoosh you hear as you flush the gas station toilet is probably because the toilet is something called pressure-assist. It uses the pressure in water supply lines to store a charge of compressed air in the tank. When you flush the toilet, the pressure is released. Pressure-assist toilets are designed to eliminate waste quickly and powerfully and to keep the bowl clean.

These fixtures make sense in high-traffic bathrooms, and under special circumstances there may be a reason to have one at home. They can use somewhat less water than a conventional toilet, for instance. But in general, modern toilets are efficient enough to work without a pressure-assist option, and this feature adds complexity to an otherwise simple device. They also tend to be more expensive than a conventional model.

Macerating Toilets

Bathrooms installed below grade are problematic from a plumbing point of view. If the outlet from the toilet is below the waste line, a standard fixture won't work. That's where a macerating toilet comes in.

Macerate means "to chop into bits," and that's exactly what these fixtures do—turn solid waste into a slurry that can be pumped through a line as small as ¾ in. diameter for disposal. Some models can pump waste 12 ft. vertically and 150 ft. horizontally, making it possible to plumb a toilet into a spot that would otherwise be inaccessible.

Even better, the toilets can be installed over any finish surface without the need for below-floor traps or plumbing. Expect to pay more for a macerating toilet than a no-frills conventional toilet.

Wall-Hung Toilets

Wall-hung toilets make it much easier to keep the bathroom floor clean, and many have shed the institutional look. Some models come with tanks that are concealed in the wall, so the toilet doesn't project into the room as far as a standard toilet.

Plumbing a wall-hung toilet is somewhat more complex because waste lines have to be roughed in differently and because the wall must carry the weight of the fixture. But a well-designed support and carrier, such as the Geberit, includes a prefabricated steel frame that pops into a standard 2x6 wall as well as other plumbing parts to simplify the job for a plumber.

They're substantially more expensive than standard floor-mounted toilets.

With nothing sitting directly on the floor, it's easy to run a broom or mop beneath a wall-mounted toilet.

Pushing the handle down on this pressure-assist toilet provides a 1.1-gal. flush; raising the handle eliminates solid waste with a 1.6-gal. flush.

Wall-mounted toilets are less bulky than conventional designs because the water tank is buried in the wall. Plumbing and installation, however, are more complex.

Toilets That Save Water

Manufacturers have long since adapted to the 1.6 gpf rule and have gone on to design toilets that use 20 percent less water, or 1.28 gpf. These are called high-efficiency toilets and meet the Environmental Protection Agency's WaterSense guidelines.

The savings can be significant. Using Toto's five-flush-per-day guideline and an average household of 3.2 people, a WaterSense toilet will save more than 1,800 gallons of water each year.

High-efficiency toilets are likely to become the new standard over time. Legislation passed in California will require them to be phased in over time with a switch to 1.28 gpf designs by 2014.

Another approach to cutting water consumption is with a dual-flush toilet, which uses a 1.6-gallon flush for solid waste and 1 gallon or less for liquid waste. Dual-flush toilets are common in Europe, Asia, and Australia, and they make a lot of sense. But the toilets start with less water in the bowl than conventional models, and anecdotally you will hear they don't always clean themselves as efficiently.

The ultimate water-saving toilet is one that doesn't use any water at all. The Clivus Multrum, developed by a Swedish engineer in 1939, was the first commercialized composting toilet, but there are now more contemporary models that look, more or less, like any other toilet and require no bulky composting chamber below the floor.

The BioLet 10, for example, uses no water, has no septic hookup, and is designed for full-time use by a household of three people (other models can handle larger crowds). Waste biodegrades quickly thanks to a fan that circulates air through the fixture and a thermostatically controlled heater that together reduce the waste volume by more than 90 percent and turns it into humus you empty every couple of months. Nonelectric models also are available. In both types, positive air flow controls odor.

Dual-flush toilets have two flush options, one for solid waste and another for liquid. These water-saving toilets have been standard in Europe for years.

Composting toilets are an obvious choice where a standard toilet is impractical, either because water is that scarce or because conventional waste disposal isn't available. Yet the compact design and nonthreatening aesthetics make them a viable choice in an everyday bathroom, too. What you save in water bills, however, will be somewhat offset by costs: the BioLet retails for about $1,800.

above · High-efficiency toilets, like this one made by American Standard, don't look any different than a conventional toilet, but they use a lot less water.

right · Composting toilets break down waste naturally. Modern designs control odor effectively.

Urinals and Bidets

It's been several years since *The New York Times* broke the news that urinals were becoming increasingly common in high-end bathrooms. If that hasn't amounted to a tidal wave of interest, urinals may yet catch on simply because they're so practical.

Urinals also are a lot more interesting visually than what you'll find in public restrooms. Philip Watts Design, Villeroy & Boch, Duravit, and Kohler offer contemporary designs. Urinals use less water than even a dual-flush toilet; waterless models also are available from several manufactures.

BIDETS

A mistake involving proper use of a bidet produced a memorable scene in Henry Miller's *Tropic of Cancer*, but it's understandable given the slow acceptance outside Europe of this French invention. Bidets are still the exception rather than the rule in American bathrooms, but they are more useful and practical than many give them credit for.

A bidet is a low basin where you can wash up after using the toilet. They're useful for both men and women, and they're available in a variety of styles from most major fixture manufacturers.

Bidets are often installed next to the toilet, so they are not practical for very small bathrooms. But where there is enough floor space, they're a sensible addition.

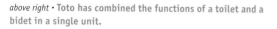

above right • Toto has combined the functions of a toilet and a bidet in a single unit.

right • Installing a bidet next to the toilet is the height of practicality, at least in a bathroom with enough floor space to accommodate them.

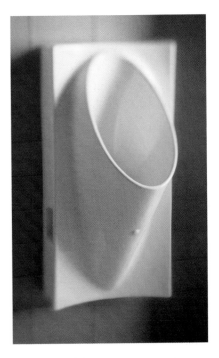

above · Urinals are a single-gender fixture, but they help to keep bathrooms cleaner, especially if there are young boys in the house.

above left · Toilet/bidet combinations can be very contemporary in design.

left · While still uncommon in the United States, bidets have a variety of hygienic advantages and can be installed next to the toilet.

Better, Not Bigger

A more thoughtful use of the existing footprint rather than an expansion improved this children's bathroom in a turn-of-the-century Victorian home.

While a simple color palette is best in a small space to keep it from feeling cluttered, it doesn't have to be stark, as is evidenced here. Understated glass accent tiles add just enough color to white subway tile wainscoting that surrounds the room and complements the light green paint.

Dark cabinet knobs and pulls as well as the tile floor seem to march the eye toward the centerpiece of the space—a new walk-in shower. It took the place of a corner tub that was rarely used. The large shower is separated from the rest of the bathroom with a frosted glass window and swinging door. The painted trim framing the window and door helps connect the shower visually with the rest of the room; inside the shower, a marble bench and shelves match the vanity top.

While new millwork helped unify the room, new cabinetry provided more storage for the three children who use the bathroom.

left and right • A row of accent tile at the top of the tile wainscoting is a simple but effective detail that picks up on the color of the painted upper walls.

above and left • A large shower replaced a seldom-used tub at one end of the renovated space. A frosted glass door and window admit plenty of light.

TUBS AND

Bathing is both pleasure and a practical necessity. Tub choices range from

deep Japanese-style soakers to period claw-foots, while showers offer

an unrivaled opportunity for custom sizes and shapes.

SHOWERS

A generation or two ago, many American households were equipped with a simple 5-ft. tub that, with a curtain, doubled as a shower. It was practical if a little predictable. These days, there is a far broader range of options in both period and contemporary styles; you can find something to match virtually any architectural style, budget, and floor plan.

Although tubs are still common, some designers are steering homeowners toward oversize custom showers instead. The impressive range of finish materials now on the market includes glass and stone tile and even pebble surfaces, making it easier for homeowners to come up with designs that are uniquely their own.

above · A tub that also can be used as a shower makes sense when there isn't enough room for two dedicated fixtures.

left · With its high back, a slipper tub is an invitation for a long soak while complementing the beadboard wainscoting and other period details.

above • Pairing a large shower with a large tub is the best of both worlds—a shower for convenience, a tub for relaxing.

left • Deep soaking tubs modeled after traditional Japanese tubs are designed for soaking in water up to the chin.

Tubs and Showers   73

Bathtubs

Showers may be fast and convenient, but you'll still find a bathtub in most American homes. Even if you choose an oversize shower instead of a tub in the master bath, at least one bathroom in the house should have a tub for washing children, for taking a long if only occasional soak, and to protect the resale value of the house.

The standard 60-in.-long tub is a minimum; it doesn't take up much room even in a smaller guest bath, and a gelcoat or acrylic shower/tub combination isn't especially expensive. There are, of course, many other options, ranging from jetted tubs and deep, Japanese-style soaking tubs to old-fashioned slipper tubs perfect in a period home and very modern tubs equipped with light-emitting diodes (LEDs), for what manufacturers call "chromatherapy." Materials run the gamut, too: plastic, porcelain over cast iron, wood, enameled steel, and copper or bronze.

There is one caveat: big tubs can get very heavy. A large tub, 4 ft. by 5 ft. and 34 in. deep, can hold more than 100 gal. of water and weigh more than a half-ton when filled. In both new construction and a renovation, make sure the floor framing is designed for this kind of load.

WHIRLPOOL TUBS

Large, jetted (or whirlpool) bathtubs have become commonplace, installed automatically by some builders because they assume buyers want them and frequently requested by homeowners in bathroom remodels. There are many brands and types on the market, but before going shopping, be realistic about whether the tub will get enough use to justify its expense and the floor space it takes up. Another consideration: does your existing hot-water heater have enough capacity to fill it?

above • Building a tub into a nook is one way of making it less obtrusive visually.

facing page, bottom • When space permits, a large soaking tub can become the focal point of the bathroom.

above • Claw-foot tubs are typically of one color, but finishing the lower half of this one in a dark color helps make it seem a little less massive.

Some homeowners love these tubs, and it's easy to see why. A soak in a whirlpool tub can do a lot to relieve the aches and pains of everyday life. Nozzles in the walls pump water against the bather for a massagelike experience. In some tubs, the jets can be adjusted for both direction and water volume. The number and location of jets varies by manufacturer. Tubs with in-line heaters will keep water at a comfortable temperature while you're relaxing.

Be aware, though, that there's some maintenance involved with owning a whirlpool. Plumbing and pumps periodically should be cleared of accumulated dirt, soap, body oils and shampoo. *Good Housekeeping* magazine recommends this procedure at least once a month, but it's pretty simple: Fill the tub with hot water, add disinfectant, and circulate water through the system.

AIR-JET TUBS

In an air-jet tub, streams of tiny bubbles instead of water are forced from small openings in the walls of the tub. Some models allow the intensity of the air streams to be adjusted, to let the bather target a sore back or tired feet, for example. Because bath water isn't circulated through the tub's internal plumbing, air-jet tubs don't need the disinfecting that whirlpools do. Some manufacturers' air-jet tubs clear the lines of any residual water automatically when the tub is drained. And air-jet tubs aren't as complex as whirlpools so they're less prone to problems.

Some users find the streams of air bubbles less intense than a water-jetted tub, and they say the air jets noticeably cool the bath water. Water-jetted tubs can overcome this problem with in-line heaters that keep tub water at a constant temperature. If you're trying to decide between the two types of jetted tubs, it would be a good idea to discuss these issues with your designer.

above right • Jetted tubs come in a variety of shapes and sizes, including models that take up no more room than a standard 60-in. bathtub.

right • Tubs may use either water or air jets, and some models combine both features in a single unit.

Soaking in a jetted tub with a view is a great way to relax. For everyday use, an adjacent shower may be more practical.

SOAKING TUBS

Bathing traditions in Japan are very different than in the U.S. The traditional soaking tub, or ofuro, is deeper than the tubs we're used to seeing. The idea behind these tubs is soaking, not washing. In fact, you climb in and relax after cleaning yourself thoroughly in an adjacent bathing area. Not all of those traditions will necessarily translate to bathrooms in the United States, but Japanese-style tubs are widely available here and made from a variety of materials. These include wood, the traditional material in Japan, as well as acrylic, stainless steel, copper, and, in a custom installation, concrete.

Like the larger whirlpool and air-jet tubs, soaking tubs can hold a lot of water, and they are deep enough to allow the bather to sit upright with water at chin height. Because their shape is not as elongated as a conventional bathtub, they don't take up as much floor area. Their depth may require either an external step or a design that sinks the tub at least partway into the floor to make it easier to get in and out.

right • In this large bathroom, the bathtub and shower each has a separate zone with a vanity and mirror between them.

above • Large windows over the tub flood this bathroom with light but can be covered with roll-down shades when privacy is required.

left • When built into a tiled surround, even a large soaking tub retreats into the background, and the tub deck provides room for towels and toiletries.

COLOR THERAPY TUBS

If an air-jet or whirlpool tub isn't soothing enough on its own, you can always move up to a bathtub that simultaneously provides color therapy, or "chromatherapy," and a gentle massage. Chromatherapy is a form of holistic medicine that uses color to promote emotional and physical well-being. Tubs with this feature incorporate light-emitting diodes that on command emit a range of colors. Controls allow the bather to choose the color that best suits his or her mood.

TUBS WITH DOORS

Older people and those with a disability may find it difficult to get in and out of a conventional bathtub. One solution is a walk-in tub with a built-in door. With the door open, the bather steps over a very low curb, takes a seat, closes the door, and fills the tub. Walk-in tubs are manufactured by several companies and available with doors that swing in or out. An in-swinging door would make more sense in a cramped bathroom where clearance is a problem. One argument against them is that the tubs are harder to exit in an emergency because all or most of the water has to drain from the tub before the door can be opened. However, in its favor, an in-swinging door is pushed against its seal by the weight of the water, making a catastrophic leak unlikely.

Walk-in tubs are typically more compact than conventional bathtubs (and also more expensive). With an integral seat, they are designed along the lines of a deep soaking tub.

above right • **Kohler and American Standard are among manufacturers that offer tubs with built-in LEDs. Colored lights are intended to promote both emotional and physical health.**

right • **A walk-in tub is ideal for someone who finds it difficult to climb in and out of a conventional bathtub. Doors may open in or out, depending on the manufacturer.**

left • The broad ledge around the lip of this tub doubles as a seat for the adjacent shower. Locating fixtures next to each other keeps all the wet in one part of the room.

above • A narrow foyer at one end of this bathroom is sized perfectly for a large built-in tub. The green ceramic tile used for the surround gives the installation some pop.

Bathtubs

Tubs are made with a variety of materials. In general, the more you spend, the more durable the tub should be. Copper, bronze, and stainless-steel fixtures are the most costly.

FIBERGLASS/GELCOAT
$

- A mold is sprayed with a thin layer of polyester resin called gelcoat, then layers of fiberglass are added for strength.
- Resists stains, but the topcoat is thinner and not as durable as other plastic options, such as acrylic.
- Follow the manufacturer's recommendations on cleaning to avoid damaging the surface.

PORCELAIN OVER STEEL
$

- Porcelain enamel is fused with heat to a substrate of sheet steel formed into a tub.
- Lighter in weight than cast-iron tubs, but not as durable.
- Porcelain is easy to keep clean and resists stains, but any nicks or cracks in the surface will allow the steel tub to rust.

ACRYLIC
$$

- Made by forming sheets of acrylic in a vacuum mold and reinforcing the tub with fiberglass.
- More durable than fiberglass/gelcoat with a thicker color layer so minor scratches won't be obvious.
- Like fiberglass/gelcoat, acrylic should not be cleaned with harsh, abrasive cleaners.

CULTURED MARBLE
$$

- Tubs are made with a mixture of marble dust and plastic resins to resemble the look of stone.
- Some manufacturers offer to make shower surrounds and sinks at the same time for a good color match throughout the bathroom.
- As with other fixtures, choose the right cleaner to avoid damaging the surface.

PORCELAIN ENAMEL OVER CAST IRON
$$-$$$

- Extremely durable but also heavy.
- Surface is nonporous, stain resistant, and easy to keep clean.
- The process in which the enamel is bonded to the cast-iron core produces deep, vivid colors.
- Mass of cast iron helps maintain water temperature.

COPPER, BRONZE, AND STAINLESS STEEL
$$$

- Very expensive, but also extremely durable.
- Retain heat like cast iron.
- Not susceptible to corrosion, but some metal surfaces require polishing to maintain their original luster.

above • A freestanding tub is more of a design element in a bathroom than a tub hidden by a surround.

left • Allowing floor tile to lap up the side of the tub surround is an effective way of making the bathroom feel cohesive.

Freestanding Tubs

Nothing complements period décor in an old house better than an old bathtub, or at least one that looks old: a claw-foot or a slipper tub. A claw-foot tub sits on decorative cast-iron feet and has exposed supply and drain lines at one end. A slipper tub is very similar, except that one end swoops up to provide a comfortable back rest. Double-ended slipper tubs are raised at each end. Yet another variation on this basic design is a pedestal tub, which has a solid pedestal instead of individual feet for support.

Vintage tubs can still be found, but reproductions in both cast iron and acrylic also are available from a number of suppliers. Claw-foot tubs are a little deeper than a standard tub and sometimes shorter, so they're not only good for a soak but also can be incorporated into a small bathroom, an advantage in many older homes. In a chilly, drafty bathroom, though, all that exposed cast iron cools bath water quickly, and because of their height, freestanding tubs are somewhat more difficult to climb into and out of, making them a second choice if you're remodeling to age in place.

above • **This contemporary soaking tub exemplifies the wide variety that's available. When choosing a tub with this much capacity, however, consider its weight, the floor framing, and the capacity of the hot-water heater.**

Refinishing an Old Tub

Porcelain enamel fired at high temperatures is a very tough finish that should last for decades if it's cleaned and cared for properly. With intense heat, the porcelain fuses with the cast iron and makes a smooth, durable surface. But it's not indestructible, and in time the porcelain can be chipped, stained, or worn away. Many an old tub has been discarded for these reasons, but it's also possible to refinish an old bathtub and bring it back to near-new condition at a much lower cost than replacement.

Repairs can be done in about a day without removing the tub. Technicians clean and prep the surface, fill any chips or surface defects, and spray on several coats of acrylic urethane enamel. The Bathtub Refinishing Association of America, a trade group, maintains a database of refinishers on its Web site that is searchable by state (www.braoa.org). Although the listings are skimpy for some states, it's a place to start.

In addition to in-place repairs, some companies remove the old finish entirely, recoat the cast iron with porcelain enamel, and fire the tub in an oven for a finish that should be nearly like the original. Because of the expense of removing, shipping, and reinstalling the tub, it would have to be special to warrant that kind of attention and may make more sense for a smaller fixture, such as a sink.

A claw-foot tub with its exposed supply valves and drain lines is a perfect complement to this period bathroom.

Borrowing Space Allows a Bath to Grow

Sam likes showers; Vivien likes baths. To make enough room for a separate shower and tub, space was borrowed from an adjacent utility room and closet to create the expanded master bath.

"The main challenge for the floor plan was space," says designer Debbie Cleary. "Luckily there was a bit of unused space on the other side of the bathroom, which I was able to take advantage of."

The enlarged space still seemed on the small side, so Cleary added a pair of windows to an exterior wall over the new tub and installed a mirror on the opposite wall to let in more light and provide views of Sam's garden outside. Cleary also used a sliding door with a translucent panel, rather than a solid, swinging door, to help the bathroom feel roomier. It's tricks like these that help a room appear larger even though the footprint of the space might not have changed.

The toilet is tucked around the corner from the door, so when you look into the bathroom you see an open, inviting space with a tub plus a view of the garden.

Vivien's choice of green, glossy tiles helps to reflect incoming natural light. Black and cream round out the simple color palette.

A pocket door replaces a standard swinging door, making the most of limited floor area.

This redesigned bath borrowed space from an adjacent utility area to make room for both a tub and a large shower.

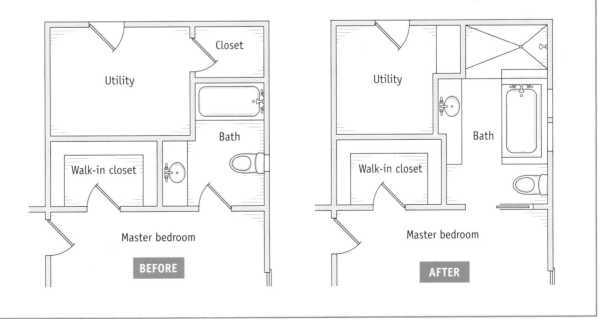

Closet

Utility

Bath

Walk-in closet

Master bedroom

BEFORE

Utility

Bath

Walk-in closet

Master bedroom

AFTER

Showers

Many designers have their doubts about the practicality of oversize whirlpool tubs; they simply don't get used as often as people expect. When Alan Asarnow, a certified master designer at the New Jersey firm of Ulrich, Inc., designs a bathroom, he starts by asking his clients whether they're in the habit of taking lengthy baths—not once in a while, but on a regular basis. If not, he suggests they consider a "really comfortable, really luxurious" shower instead. More homeowners seem to be taking the point. Oversize showers with built-in nooks for toiletries plus a seat or bench are more common than ever in large master baths, and custom showers are often paired with jetted or soaking tubs.

Inventive designers have helped reshape a standard shower into something far more interesting. Stone and ceramic tile, colorful glass mosaics, glass block, and sheets of tempered glass all have the potential to make showers seem light, airy, and spacious. Some showers in master baths are quite large, big enough to accommodate two people. Even when the footprint is small, careful materials selection can make these showers the focal point of the bathroom.

A shower need not be huge to be useful. Whether they are manufactured units or made on-site with a standard tub and a tile surround, combination tub/showers will probably remain a mainstay in many American homes. They meld two essentials in a single, moderately priced fixture that doesn't take up much space. They're an obvious choice in smaller homes where there isn't enough room for a separate tub and shower. And even if many people opt for a quick shower instead of using the tub, it's not a good idea to do away with a tub altogether. Families with small children need a tub, and almost anyone could use a therapeutic soak once in a while. For these reasons, combination tub/showers are an option worth exploring if only for a guest bath.

left • Minimal glass walls and an oversize panel of opaque glass help blend this inviting shower seamlessly into the room.

below • A full-height glass panel separates inside and outside showers at a house where backyard privacy isn't a concern.

A window with frosted glass provides privacy yet still admits lots of natural light into this oversized shower. The transom light above has clear glazing.

EASY-ACCESS SHOWERS

Some of the most appealing shower designs are curbless, easy-access showers that are integrated with the rest of the bathroom; that is, no curb, no curtain, and no wall between the shower and the rest of the room. Showers like these take extra planning because the entire bathroom floor, or at least a good portion of it, becomes an extra-large shower pan that must be watertight. Curbless showers are an important feature of accessible-design bathrooms, covered in more detail on pp. 20–29.

Visually, curbless showers help a bathroom get beyond a sense of compartmentalization and thus seem larger and more relaxed.

Unlike conventional tub and shower combination units that come in standard sizes, there's no set formula for an easy-access shower. The exact dimensions and layout are obviously dependent on the overall size of the bathroom but also on how much of the floor space you want to turn into a wet area. Even very small bathrooms can incorporate curbless showers when the whole room becomes, in effect, the shower pan with a centrally located drain that serves the whole floor.

It may be more practical to set aside a portion of the room and use a partial wall to keep water from splashing all over the room. Or, as in the case of the photo at right, a wall can define a bathing area that includes both a curbless shower and a tub.

In a conventional shower, only the shower pan itself must be sloped to direct water to the drain. In curbless designs, this gets a little more complicated because the floor of the shower area must be lower than the floor in the balance of the room. It's that or have shower water creeping under the door and down the hall. This is not a standard detail and will require extra planning on the part of the framer and is a detail much better suited to new construction than a renovation.

Incorporating a curbless shower requires a conversation with the builder very early in the construction process so he can plan appropriately. The time to broach the idea is not when the floor has been framed and the plumber or tile setter is about to start work.

above · Without a conventional curb, this shower is barrier free. A vertical panel limits splashing, but even if some water escapes, the tile floor can handle it.

left · A gracefully curved wall divides the bathing area from the rest of the bathroom. Water drains from a central point in the wet area, thanks to a carefully pitched floor.

right · A combination of natural stone and ceramic tile makes this shower an inviting corner of the bathroom. The change in tile used for the shower floor is repeated throughout the shower space, helping it to feel cohesive even while it's open to the room.

Combination Tub/Showers

Combination tub/showers can be purchased as manufactured plastic units or assembled on-site from a tub and a tile surround. In period homes, a simple curtain rod encircling a claw-foot tub may be all that's required. Of the many options, manufactured combination tub/showers are somewhat easier to keep clean and require less maintenance, thanks to their full-height walls that minimize the risk of water damage. Tiled shower surrounds, however, offer a much greater opportunity for creative mixes of color and texture.

right • An old-fashioned tub, china console, and coordinating fabric shower curtain and window treatment together spell period bathroom.

DETAILS THAT WORK

Built-In Storage

With a little forethought, a shallow niche built into the wall offers a convenient place for storing clean towels and a tilt-out hamper for dirty clothes.

left • Combining a bathtub and shower is a good option in a household with small children and when space is tight. Manufactured plastic fixtures are economical and readily available. Another option is a conventional tub with a tile surround.

Simple can be appealing, too. White subway tiles installed vertically complement the beadboard wainscoting and make a clean, easy-to-care-for surface.

Niches

For a few bucks you can buy a wire rack and hang it over the shower arm to store soap and shampoo. It's perfectly serviceable, but shower niches are neater and take up less room. Recessed into the shower wall, a niche can incorporate one or more shelves and tile or stone that contrasts in color or texture with the rest of the shower.

Niches are set between studs in the wall framing and can be built to a custom size or purchased as a preformed insert. However it's done, keeping the installation waterproof is essential. A leaky niche will allow water to get behind the tile backerboard and cause long-term problems, so the tile setter has to take care in choosing the right materials and installing them correctly. Several manufacturers offer specialty products for this purpose.

The tiler also should lay out the niche so its edges line up with grout lines in the rest of the tile wall; this is more finished looking than having the sides of the niche land haphazardly on the field tile. If that's not possible, a border can help make the problem go away.

1. Using a contrasting color and tile size in the back wall of this niche helps it stand out from the field tiles in the shower wall.
2. The more gentle contrast in color and the lack of a border around the edge gives this niche an entirely different look. 3. Niches offer an opportunity for creativity and don't have to be strictly rectilinear.
4. A horizontal niche over a tub is accentuated by a pattern of different tile shapes and sizes. 5. This shallow niche was designed to blend in with the wall. 6. More generously sized niches can store more than toiletries. Glass shelves keep the overall feel light.

Showerheads

If bath designers are squeezing more potential out of the shower, they're getting a boost from manufacturers who make faucets, showerheads, and other controls. While federal law limits the volume of water that can be delivered by a single fixture to 2.5 gallons per minute, the variety of water delivery options has grown substantially. In addition to the utilitarian water-saver showerhead, there are oversize showerheads that mimic rainfall, multifunction showerheads, and handheld showers, all of which offer more versatility.

A single shower equipped with multiple showerheads uses a lot of water, but some people like them nonetheless. Installing several showerheads is one way of skirting the federal edict on water consumption.

A practical argument in favor of a multihead setup is in a bathroom that will be used by someone who uses a wheelchair or needs to shower while seated. Having a showerhead at a lower-than-standard height, in addition to a conventionally located showerhead, also would be useful for children. As long as the heads aren't being used at the same time there's no net gain in water consumption, so no foul on the conservation front.

If you're planning on this kind of shower, make sure to talk about it with your plumber well in advance, while there's still time to run extra supply lines to the bathroom. Running more than one showerhead from a single, standard-size supply line will produce more dribble than pizzazz. Also, check with your plumber whether the size of the water heater should be increased to handle the added load. These big "performance showers," as they are called, consume hot water at two or three times that of a normal shower, so you might need a dedicated hot water heater.

above • Showers with a number of water outlets are not uncommon, but they require a water heater and water-supply lines that can handle the load. If water conservation is a concern, skip it altogether.

above • Showerheads can be sculptural in shape.

above • An oversized showerhead and a single control make a simple, uncluttered installation.

above • Two showerheads provide dual action. The large showerhead delivers a gentle rainlike spray, while the smaller one in the background provides a more brisk pattern.

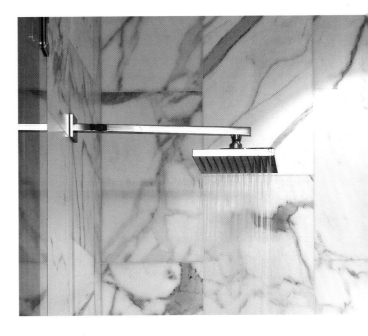

above • This square showerhead delivers a gentle spray pattern.

Finding Space under the Eaves

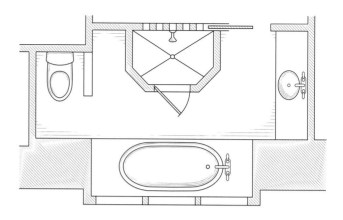

The new owners of a long, narrow carriage house in Philadelphia wanted to modernize the house without degrading its 19th-century charm or making its footprint any bigger.

To create more space on the second floor for a reworked master bedroom and bath, Krieger + Associates Architects added eight new shed dormers to the roof. By borrowing some room from the existing master bedroom and a closet, the plan cleared the way for a new, 15-ft.-long master bath.

A dormer at the center of the room provided ample headroom for a large tub and a shower. The glass shower enclosure helps keep the room from seeming small.

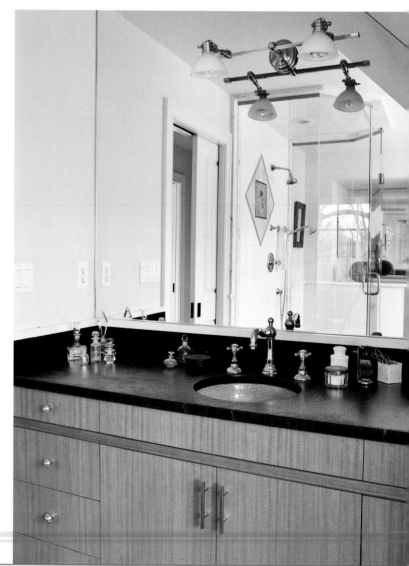

The sink vanity and toilet are located at opposite ends of the room, outside the bounds of the dormer, where headroom is limited. Instead of enclosing the toilet behind a door, the architects separated it from the rest of the bathroom with a half wall that provides some privacy. A glass panel behind the toilet helps to brighten the corner.

To heat the new bathroom, Krieger considered several low-profile radiators but were reluctant to give up any wall space or make any compromises on appearance. Their solution was a pair of Myson towel warmers that could be mounted on the granite deck of the tub. In addition to a small section of baseboard heat near the toilet, the hydronic warmers have enough output to keep the room comfortable.

The new vanity occupies a niche on one side of the room. A large mirror reflects light from dormer windows and helps the room feel spacious.

above • A pocket door entry minimizes the loss of floor space in this narrow area.

above • Hydronic towel warmers provide enough heat to supplement a small baseboard heater. Plus, they're beautiful and practical.

left • A half wall separates the toilet from the rest of the bathroom. The large stone and glass panel add texture and color.

FLOORS,

Finish materials for bathroom floors, walls,

and ceilings include everything from wood to glass tile.

WALLS &

Durability and water resistance are key,

while color and texture can help define the room.

CEILINGS

With the possible exception of the kitchen, nowhere in the house do surface materials get a tougher workout than in the bathroom. There not only is a lot of foot traffic and wear and tear that comes with constant use, but also an unending exposure to surface water and high humidity.

In choosing finish materials for floors, walls, and ceilings, durability and water resistance are more important than anything else. Yet these surfaces also play a key visual role, making color and texture important considerations as well.

The great variety of materials on the market makes it possible to get both high performance and the right look. Although it's certainly possible to spend a lot of money on high-end materials, it's not absolutely necessary.

above • Hand-painted surfaces are unique. Although more expensive than conventional finishes, a mural is an opportunity for creativity and fun.

above right • Wood has certain drawbacks as a finish material in the bathroom, particularly for flooring. But there's no denying its visual warmth, and it's often a perfect match in period or less formal homes.

right • Texture is key in this combination of pebbled surfaces on both the wall and floor. The walls need no further decoration.

facing page • Multicolored tiles used on both the floor and walls of this bathroom are a powerful unifier. A spare vanity with an open base lets the tile take center stage.

Floors

The best bathroom floors are impervious to water, hold up well to wear and tear, and have enough texture so they're not overly slippery when wet.

A number of materials can make that claim but none more convincingly than porcelain or ceramic tile and natural stone. Neither should ever wear out, at least in the conventional sense of the word, and will succumb to changes in fashion far sooner than to damage from daily use.

With the exception of bath mats or modestly sized throw rugs, carpet is about the only conventional floor covering that should absolutely be avoided in the bathroom. Just about anything else is worth considering, depending on your budget and particular circumstances. That leaves vinyl, linoleum, wood and engineered wood, cork, and laminate. None of them really measures up to stone or tile for a bathroom, but they all have something to offer, often at a lower price.

Wood flooring is warm underfoot, but the finish must be maintained scrupulously, especially around a tub or shower, to prevent water damage.

Flooring

Water resistance is key, but especially in a bathroom where splashing in the tub or at the sink is expected, such as in a child's bath. If that's not likely, color and texture may be more important considerations. In all categories of flooring, prices vary widely. Basic ceramic tile, for example, is available at relatively low prices at home centers or tile stores, while some glass and art tile can get very pricey.

VINYL
$

- Comfortable underfoot.
- Great variety in patterns and colors.
- Relatively inexpensive but not as durable as stone or ceramic tile.
- If choosing vinyl, look for "inlaid" material, meaning the color goes all the way through the flooring.
- Available in tile and plank form as well as sheets.
- Highly stain resistant and impervious to water.
- Softeners called phthalates pose health risks, according to some environmental groups.
- Vinyl tile can be installed by DIYers, but where standing water is likely, choose sheet vinyl to minimize the number of seams.

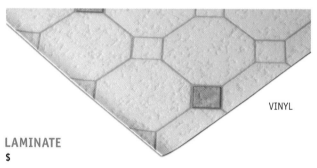

VINYL

LAMINATE
$

- Snap-together installation is fast.
- Inexpensive.
- Sold in many wood look-alike patterns.
- Top wear layer is durable, but fiberboard core will swell when exposed to water damage so use around tubs, toilets, and sinks with caution and keep all perimeter edges caulked and sealed.
- Standing water needs to be cleaned up promptly.

WOOD

WOOD
$-$$

- Warm underfoot.
- Can be stained to virtually any color.
- Visually appealing and well suited for period homes.
- Can be purchased prefinished.
- Not a good choice around tubs, sinks, and toilets unless the finish is maintained and edges are caulked and sealed.
- Shrinks and expands seasonally with changes in indoor humidity. Gaps between individual planks can widen in winter, and boards may cup in summer if the flooring is laid too tightly.

ENGINEERED WOOD
$$

- Made from a layer of wood over a plywood core.
- Same advantages as solid wood flooring, but more dimensionally stable and less likely to shrink and expand with changes in humidity.
- Can be purchased prefinished, but water resistance will be higher if finished after installation.
- Like solid wood, not the best choice in a bathroom if frequent wetting and standing water are likely.

STONE
$$-$$$

- Long-wearing natural material with great visual appeal.
- Wide range of colors and textures on the market.
- Some polished stone is very slippery when wet.
- Thick stone may require heavier than usual floor framing.
- Most types of stone should be sealed periodically to prevent stains.
- Grout between stones may stain if left unsealed.

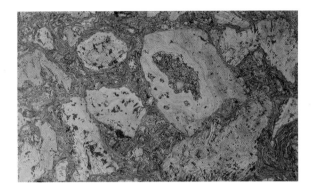

CORK

CORK AND LINOLEUM
$$

- Resilient flooring with better environmental credits than vinyl.
- Warm and forgiving underfoot.
- Made mostly from natural and benign materials. Cork, for example, is sustainably harvested bark of the cork oak.
- Naturally biodegradable.
- Available in tile and sheet form.
- More expensive than vinyl and requires more care.

TILE

TILE
$-$$

- Huge variety in color, texture, and surface appearance.
- Offers great design flexibility.
- Extremely durable.
- Very low maintenance.
- Ceramic and porcelain tiles are resistant to stains and moisture.
- Requires stiff floor framing to prevent cracking.
- Without source of heat below, it is cold underfoot.
- Grout should be sealed to prevent stains and mildew.

TILE

Few materials make more sense in the bathroom than tile. Its broad range of colors, sizes, and patterns, combined with its water and stain resistance and durability, all help make it a good choice.

Tiles of different colors or sizes can be combined in the same floor—a white-and-black checkerboard, for example, or a mosaic pattern set in a plain field—making this material extremely versatile from a design standpoint. Introducing a few fancy tiles in an otherwise plain floor is one way of jazzing up the room at a relatively low cost. In an older house, a skillful tile-setter can help camouflage out-of-square corners or uneven walls.

Ceramic and porcelain tile are fired at high temperatures, making them highly resistant to water absorption and stains. Unglazed terra-cotta tile, on the other hand, is much more porous and should be sealed to keep out water.

One thing tile doesn't like is too much flex in the floor. The larger the tile, the greater the risk of cracking. In an older home, where floor framing is sometimes undersized, an existing floor may have too much bounce. In that case, floor joists may need reinforcement before a tile floor can be installed successfully. Special membranes, such as Schluter®-Ditra, installed between the tile and the subflooring can help isolate tile, or "uncouple" it, from damaging movement in the substrate.

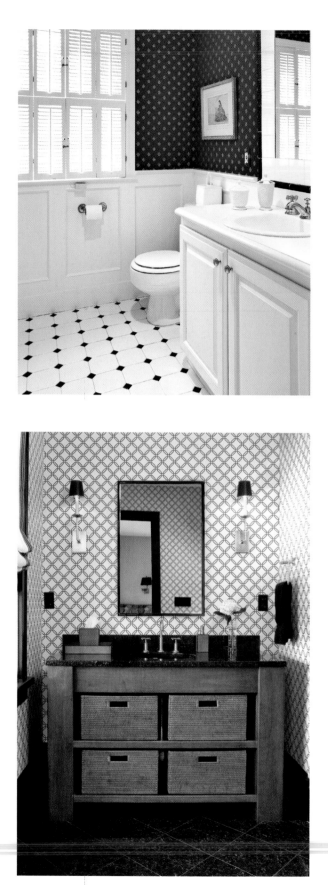

above right · White ceramic tile with contrasting squares set at each corner make an attractive surface that's relatively easy to create.

right · Tile laid in a diagonal pattern can help make a smaller space seem larger.

above • Large ceramic tile in different sizes can look like stone. Choosing tile of the same color for the shower walls and ceiling helps pull the room together.

left • One of the greatest advantages of tile is its versatility. Different sizes and shapes can be combined to create virtually any effect, such as this woven carpetlike pattern encircled with a dark border.

Tile doesn't require much if any maintenance beyond regular cleaning, and its hard, nonporous surface makes that a fairly simple process. Grout, however, is another story. Unlike the surface of tile itself, grouts containing sand will absorb water and can stain or support the growth of mildew. Grout lines should be sealed, and periodically resealed, to prevent these problems.

Should a tile crack or chip, which can happen even though tile is very durable, it can be replaced without disturbing the remainder of the floor. This is a real advantage, but only if a replacement tile of the same color is available. Because tile manufacturers may not always carry the exact same color or pattern, it's a good idea to tuck a few spares away when the tile is originally set.

The biggest drawback to tile is that it can be slippery when wet. If that's a special concern, look for tile with a high coefficient of friction, or COF. The higher the number, the more resistant the surface is to slips. The American with Disabilities Act suggests a minimum COF of 0.6.

above right · **This deep green floor tile helps the room feel grounded, but dark tile doesn't reflect as much light as white and off-white tile, a consideration in a small room without much natural light.**

right · **Mosaic tile used on both floor and wall gives this bath a unified, cohesive feeling, an effect that's amplified by a complementary color on the vanity.**

facing page, left · **Tile can be its own rug. Patterns created with accent tile in the center of the room and the toilet room have the appeal of a throw rug but zero chance of mold or water damage.**

above • These large, rectangular tiles have a slab-like appearance and balance the lighter colors elsewhere in the room.

Keeping Tile Warm

Tile and stone floors can be cold underfoot, appealing on a hot summer day but not so nice in January. Houses heated with radiant-floor hot water systems won't have this problem, and a good substitute in homes with more conventional heating systems is an electric mat beneath the tile surface.

These mats contain a grid of electrical wires that are controlled by a thermostat or timer. Mats, like those made by Nuheat™, are bedded in a layer of thinset adhesive with the tile installed on top of that. They're relatively inexpensive to run, especially when used for short periods of time after a bath or shower.

Installing an electric heating mat can be a DIY project, but always consult a professional to make sure wiring is done correctly and to code.

Making an Old Space Feel Modern

In new construction, spacious and efficient bathrooms can be worked into the house from the start. But in existing houses, bathrooms sometimes need an imaginative redesign to become truly functional.

A greenhouse addition to an antique cape in Falmouth, Maine, presented that kind of challenge for Whipple-Callender Architects. The homeowners loved the old part of the house, but the addition, which had been remodeled to house the kitchen and master bathroom, wasn't working. Not only was the master bath on a balcony that overlooked the kitchen, but the old greenhouse cum living space provided little in the way of thermal or acoustical insulation from the elements.

For their redesigned master bath, the owners asked for double sinks, a soaking tub, and a large shower—things that would typically be included in a newly constructed master bath. The bathroom had to be accessible from the bedroom as well as a sleeping porch, and while the owners wanted a view of the ocean, they also needed privacy from a nearby yacht club. They liked the feel of a Maine cottage and suggested using beadboard wainscoting to help create the effect.

The renovated bathroom has all that and more. While it still overlooks an open family space below, there is more privacy and a better connection to both a dressing room and nearby master bedroom. A glassed shower provides views across the room toward the ocean.

The architects started with a marble mosaic floor tile and found a coordinating green wall tile that was made to look just like beadboard, giving the owners the look they were after in a more durable material that needs less maintenance. The new bathroom is a peaceful place, with a mix of modern and traditional parts and materials that are delightfully cohesive.

right · Wall tile that looks like beadboard, used for both the tub surround and wainscoting, helps create an informal cottage flavor in this Falmouth, Maine, master bath.

facing page, top · A full-width mirror over the vanity, complemented by graceful pendant lights, reflects incoming light and helps the room seem spacious.

facing page, bottom · The mosaic floor tile picks up colors in the tile wainscoting and tub surround as well as the trim.

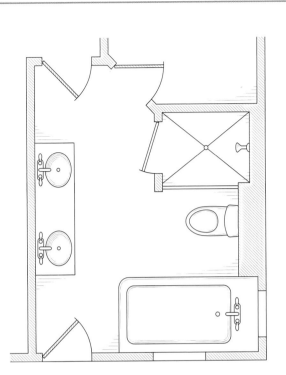

The reworked bathroom includes a double-sink vanity, separate shower and tub, and easy access to an adjacent dressing room and bedroom.

STONE

Stone has many of the same attributes as tile: it's hard, wear resistant, and available in many colors and textures.

One of the most likable characteristics of stone is its natural variegation and unpredictability, which gives it a rich and lively appearance unmatched by man-made materials. A broad range of colors is available, from the light hues of limestone to dark gray of blue slate, so the impact on the rest of the room is very flexible. Light-colored floors help make a room feel spacious and open, while dark stone often has a more formal look.

If you're interested in building green, look for stone that is quarried regionally if not locally to keep costs and the environmental impact of transportation to a minimum.

Like tile, stone can be a mix-and-match installation, with one color on the floor and another in a shower or two types of stone combined in a pattern on the floor.

Stone is more expensive than basic ceramic tile, and most should be sealed to keep out water and stains. Also, stone, like tile, is intolerant of too much flex in the floor. Where tile can be laid over a floor with a maximum deflection of 1/360 (that is, maximum sag in the middle of the floor equals the width of the floor divided by 360), stone often requires an even stiffer assembly, more so the larger the stone pieces. Thick pieces of stone set in a mortar bed may need extra floor framing, joists set at 12 in. on center, for example, rather than the more typical 16 in. on center. It's an issue to discuss well in advance with your builder.

above • Earthy and unmistakable, small river rock makes an appealing floor surface that's less formal and more organic than polished stone. A variety of rock types are available on a mesh backing, simplifying installation even for DIYers.

right • A pebbled surface can be combined with ceramic tile, like this black path in a field of white.

Stone surfaces have natural variations in color that manufactured materials can only mimic. Certain types of stone, such as slate, also have a rough texture that makes them less slippery when wet.

SOLID WOOD AND ENGINEERED WOOD

Like stone, wood is a completely natural material whose variations in color and texture are a big part of its appeal. Wood flooring is available in dozens of domestic and imported species, all with their own colors and personalities. Flooring is manufactured in solid plank form and as a more stable engineered material consisting of plywoodlike laminations that are glued together.

Solid wood has a number of practical strengths in addition to its appearance. It's resilient and warm underfoot, and because it's more flexible than stone or tile, it won't crack when installed over subflooring with a little bounce. Wood can be sanded and refinished to produce a completely fresh surface, and it can easily be cut and shaped to fit out-of-square rooms.

Wood flooring has two principal disadvantages: it shrinks and expands with changes in humidity,

meaning that gaps between individual planks will grow and shrink seasonally, and it's susceptible to water damage. Unless the surface is well sealed, water will discolor and eventually cause decay. Wood around a shower or toilet also may buckle when continually exposed to moisture.

Engineered wood is more seasonally stable than solid wood but it, too, has many of the same drawbacks when it comes to standing water. In addition, surface plies are relatively thin so it can be sanded and refinished fewer times than solid wood.

Bamboo is another form of engineered wood flooring, even though it's technically not a wood species. While dimensionally stable, it carries the same risks as any other form of wood when used in the bathroom.

CORK AND LINOLEUM

As interest in green products has increased, both cork and linoleum have started to look more appealing. Cork is a totally natural material; it is the bark of the cork oak tree that is harvested periodically without damaging the tree. It's resilient underfoot, thanks to the tiny air bubbles it contains, and is a good thermal insulator as well as sound deadener.

Vinyl flooring nearly killed the linoleum industry, but linoleum is making a comeback and is now manufactured by several companies. Linoleum is a mix of linseed oil, wood flour, and other fairly benign materials on a jute backing. Like cork, it comes in a variety of forms (plank, sheet, and tile).

Both cork and linoleum need more care than sheet vinyl, ceramic tile, or stone. Both should be well sealed against water to prevent damage. In the bathroom, choose an installation method that minimizes seams.

below • Whether it's solid wood or engineered flooring, make sure the surface is sealed with a quality floor finish and that edges abutting showers, tubs, and toilets are well caulked.

above • Paired with a classic claw-foot bathtub, a pine floor creates a soothing period look. Because pine is relatively soft, it will collect nicks and dings over time.

facing page • Wood can be stained to virtually any color. The deep red-browns of this floor anchor the room.

VINYL AND LAMINATE

While available in several grades, vinyl and laminate flooring are at the low end of the cost range. Both have some practical advantages, but neither is likely to last as long as several other flooring options. Improved manufacturing techniques allow these man-made surfaces to give more realistic impersonations of stone and other materials. But in the end, they don't look as natural as the real thing.

Of the two, vinyl is a better bet for a bathroom floor from a performance standpoint, mainly because the surface is un-affected by water and, at least in sheet form, the floor doesn't present many cracks and crevices where water can collect. In better grades of vinyl, the pattern or color goes all the way through the material—called inlaid—so even in high-traffic areas wear won't be as obvious.

One concern with vinyl flooring is chemical additives called phthalates. While they improve the working properties of the plastic, some health activists and researchers suspect these chemicals cause unwanted health consequences. (A study in 2009 raised the possibility of a connection between vinyl floor-ing and a higher than expected rate of autism among a group of children in Sweden.) Some environmental and health groups would like to see a total ban on polyvinyl chloride (PVC) products. Given the uncertainties, it's probably a good idea to look for a different type of flooring in a household where toddlers crawl around on the floors.

Laminate flooring consists of a layer of plastic over a man-made substrate like fiberboard. A printed film layer gives flooring the look of another material, such as stone or tile. Laminate flooring is a "floating" floor system, meaning it's not glued or nailed to the subfloor. Most types have tongue-and-groove edges that snap together without glue.

Manufacturers have done a lot to improve the appearance of laminate flooring, but the fiberboard core will swell if it gets wet, so a certain amount of care should be taken if this flooring is used in a bathroom. All perimeter seams should be well caulked, and water shouldn't be allowed to stand on the floor for any length of time. For these reasons, it's not the best choice in a child's bathroom.

above • Like other resilient flooring materials, vinyl flooring compresses a bit when walked on, making it feel good underfoot. One advantage to sheet vinyl over vinyl tiles is a lack of seams that would allow water intrusion.

above • Laminate flooring (right) can be made to look like natural wood, but it can be damaged if the inner core gets wet. Vinyl flooring also comes in tiles (left), but the added number of seams increases the risk of water damage.

left • Vinyl flooring can be manufactured to have the look of tile but comes with a lower initial cost; it also requires very little maintenance.

Walls and Ceilings

Finish surfaces for walls don't take quite the abuse that flooring does, but it's still important to choose materials that are durable, resistant to moisture, and easy to clean. Choices include painted or wallpapered drywall, plaster, tile, and wood.

A key factor is how the bathroom will be used. What makes sense in a powder room used only occasionally, and often by guests, probably won't be the first choice in a child's bath. In one, appearance is everything; in the other, it's all about performance.

Unless something special is planned for the ceiling—a coffered wood ceiling, for instance—moisture-resistant drywall, or possibly plaster, makes an excellent choice. A ceiling doesn't have to be especially impact resistant, and as long as the bathroom has a good fan for ventilation, these materials will be more than durable enough.

above • Painted surfaces can be as bold as you like. The colorful drawing of a fish is a perfect complement to the vivid green of these bathroom walls.

above • Wallpaper isn't as popular as it once was, yet the enormous variety of available patterns and colors makes it a good choice in a period home.

above • Paneled wainscoting with a striking red border has a look that is both traditional and lively. Paired with a stone tile floor, these surfaces will prove durable and easy to maintain.

Mosaic tile is typically found on the floor, but it also makes a durable, low-maintenance wall covering the bathroom.

When renovating a bathroom, it's sometimes a tough decision to repair versus replace wall and ceiling surfaces. Demolition makes a mess, not only in the bathroom but also, potentially, in the rest of the house, and it adds to the length and complexity of the job.

There's often a good reason, though, to strip the room to the framing. In older homes, the insulation in exterior walls is often inadequate. Moisture migrating into wall cavities over the years may well have promoted mold or even resulted in structural decay of framing or sheathing. Tearing out surface materials presents an opportunity to insulate correctly and to add an air barrier that prevents moisture from getting in.

above · Mosaic tiles covering the floor and much of the wall area make a water-resistant, easy-to-clean surface.

left · Patterned wallpaper can bring a theme to the room in a way that paint, tile, or wood can't.

facing page · Wallpaper is not the most robust of finish surfaces, but in a gently used space it should be fine. Here, in combination with wide baseboards and elegant light sconces, it imparts a slightly formal feel.

Tearing out also allows wiring upgrades—adding receptacles, for example, or replacing old cable that lacks a separate ground circuit. Removing the ceiling makes it easy to enhance lighting and to add a fan that's vented to the outside if the bathroom doesn't have one already.

Historically valuable architectural details or rare tile would, of course, change the equation. But in most cases, tearing out the old almost always makes for a more satisfying result in the end.

above • This beadboard wainscoting, more durable than the drywall on the upper part of the wall, is available in sheets made of medium-density fiberboard for speedy installation.

left • Decorative wallpaper can be a good choice for a powder room, where daily wear and tear is not an issue.

above • An elaborate cap at the top of the tile wainscoting runs all the way around the room and into the adjoining water closet, helping to link the spaces together.

left • Tile doesn't have to be bland or formal. The great diversity of colors and sizes makes custom designs possible.

Walls and Ceilings

DRYWALL
$

- Relatively inexpensive and installation can be handled by a DIYer.
- Can be repainted, making it easy to change the appearance of the room with minimal effort.
- Not a very robust surface, but can be repaired.
- Use water-resistant board to minimize the risk of damage from moisture.
- Not appropriate for use in showers and tub surrounds.

PLASTER
$$

- A more expensive option than drywall.
- Skilled labor to apply may be hard to find locally.
- Makes a hard, durable finish.
- Surface can range from textured to glassy smooth.

TILE AND STONE
$-$$$

- Very durable.
- Excellent variety in colors and textures.
- Won't be damaged by water, so it can be used in showers and on tub surrounds.
- Grout should be sealed.
- Nonporous tile surfaces are easy to keep clean.

WOOD AND WOOD LOOK-ALIKES
$-$$

- Good durability, providing it is painted or sealed and the surface is maintained.
- Fairly easy to repair if damaged and easy to refinish.
- Can be installed as tongue-and-groove planks, flat panels, or wainscoting.
- May be damaged in high-moisture areas. Not the best choice for a tub or shower surround.

left · This antique patterned wallpaper with a floral motif seems apt in a room featuring wainscoting with chair rail, a curved arch marking the tub area, and deeply profiled window and door trim.

right · Paneled wainscoting helps give this bathroom a more formal look than a plain painted wall, and it can be fabricated on site by a good finish carpenter.

below · This bathroom would look stark and austere if it weren't for the band of blue-green tile that complements the vanity top.

TILE AND STONE

One of the greatest attributes of tile is its versatility. Combining different sizes, shapes, and colors (and there are tons to choose from) can produce dazzling and completely unique effects. Although tile can get pricey, strategically placing a few handmade or brightly colored tiles in a plain field is a good way of dressing up a room at minimal expense.

right • Bright and practical, the wainscoting of yellow tile—with a durable, easy-to-clean surface—protects the walls where they're most vulnerable.

below • Translucent glass subway tile in this bathing area will keep moisture damage to walls safely at bay.

Vegas-Inspired Wild Tile

While tile can be strictly geometric and formal, it also has the power to dazzle.

The vibrant tile work in this bathroom reflects the owners' appreciation for the bright tile work they had seen in the entry of the Wynn Hotel and Casino in Las Vegas.

The young couple that owns the house travels frequently. But with two young children, that was becoming more problematic. Their idea was to make their own home fun and engaging, as attractive as any distant travel destination. This bathroom is next to a home entertainment zone, making the bright colors and organic patterns seem completely appropriate.

Designer Maraya Droney and Rick Skalak of Vita Nova Mosaic (the same tile company that did all the mosaics in the Wynn) put a twist in the Las Vegas design by using Black Galaxy granite as the background for the floor mosaics instead of the White Spider marble at the Wynn. Skalak says his company uses only American-made glass, Spectrum and Uroboros, which is guaranteed to have no lead content.

above • The bright above-counter sink complements the colors in the complex mosaic pattern in the walls and floors.

left • The entry of the Wynn Hotel and Casino in Las Vegas was the inspiration for the tile work in a bathroom next to a home entertainment area.

Tiled walls (or at least tiled wainscoting) also offer major practical advantages. Glazed ceramic tile protects a wall from water damage, and it's easy to keep clean. Stone tile has a solid, traditional feel with many of the same advantages.

In determining the height of wainscoting, tile experts Lane and Tom Meehan, authors of *Working with Tile*, suggest the top of the wainscoting be aligned with the top of the vanity backsplash. A chair rail at this height extending all the way around the room makes what they call a "comfortable horizontal focal point" and ties the room together visually. They add, however, to lay out wainscoting carefully so any decorative chair rail stays away from electrical outlets, shower mixing valves, and other obstructions.

above • A brightly colored tile wall is the focal point of this bathroom. A lack of color elsewhere helps the wall stand out.

left • Small blue tiles in the backsplash reflect the color of the walls in the adjoining bedroom and add just enough color to this small, monochromatic bathroom.

facing page • Blending different colored stone and tile creates an elegant setting in this bathroom.

WOOD AND WOOD LOOK-ALIKES

Like tile, wood has many faces. Nothing is more elegant than frame-and-panel wainscoting in mahogany or cherry; nothing more down-home than knotty pine tongue-and-groove planks. High-end work should be left to the pros, but wood can be one of the easiest of installations for do-it-yourselfers.

If you're going to paint wood, choose clear grades of lumber. No knots. Even when sealing primers are used over knotty softwood such as pine or spruce, the resins have a way of leaching through. Many species of woods are beautiful in their own right and need no dressing up beyond a good-quality sealer. The warm tones of Douglas fir, cherry, or mahogany or the cool colors of light woods such as birch or maple can become an important design element.

In addition to solid wood, plywood paneling and wood look-alikes, such as medium-density fiberboard (MDF), are other options. With marine-grade finishes, plywood can stand up to high-moisture environments. MDF beadboard is very smooth and makes an excellent painted surface. Be more careful with this kind of paneling in areas that get wet, though—it doesn't tolerate moisture well.

At its simplest, wood is a friendly material reminiscent of summer houses and casual living. If the owners ever tire of all the wood, walls would be easy to paint.

above · Beadboard walls are a good match with the classic claw-foot tub, making the space seem casual and cottagelike.

left · Tongue-and-groove paneling, along with an unpainted wood ceiling, makes an unobtrusive and economical surface. Horizontal installation on the walls stretches the space around the tub.

Floors, Walls & Ceilings   131

Borrowing Light from the Room Next Door

A remodel in San Francisco included an addition at the rear of the house, turning what had been an exterior wall into an interior wall. That alteration could have left this small bathroom dark and uninviting, but adding an interior window of opaque glass opening to an adjacent office provided a source of natural light.

The window is aligned with a mirror-fronted cabinet on the wall over the toilet and vanity, a strong design element of the room. The cabinet provides a good deal of storage, and a cove on top holds an additional source of light. Helping to maintain an open feeling is the floor-to-ceiling sheet of glass surrounding the curbless shower. A dropped ceiling over the shower helps to define the bathing area visually.

Plywood treated with marine-grade epoxy covers the walls of the bathroom. Although the choice may seem unusual, architect Eliza Hart says one of the main features of the house is wood, plywood in particular. It's used in a bookshelf at the bottom of the stairs and in the office outside this bathroom in the form of cabinets and desks. The continuity of materials helps make different spaces feel connected.

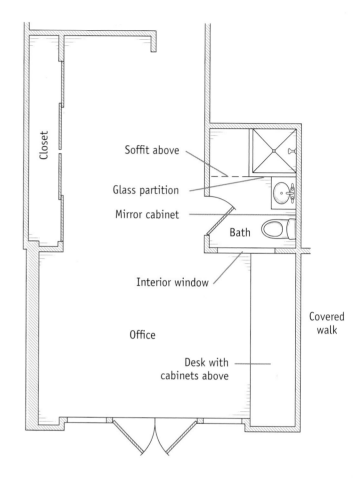

Closet

Soffit above

Glass partition

Mirror cabinet

Bath

Interior window

Office

Covered walk

Desk with cabinets above

above • Wall-mounted faucets over a concrete vanity top make for a clean, uncluttered look. The vanity is wall-hung.

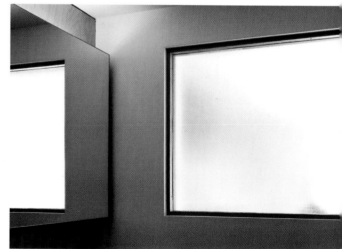

above • A window of opaque glass between the bathroom and an adjacent office is a source of natural light for this landlocked room.

Plywood walls finished with marine-grade epoxy help connect the bathroom with other parts of the house. A floor-to-ceiling sheet of glass defines one side of the curbless shower.

LIGHTING

Natural and artificial sources are both important to bathroom lighting.

When it comes to choosing fixtures, where they are placed

can be just as important as what type of bulb they use.

Good bathroom lighting, like well-designed kitchen lighting, doesn't rely on a single light source or type of fixture. It takes several kinds of lighting to make the room both functional and interesting: general (or ambient) lighting for illuminating the entire room, task lighting for applying makeup or shaving, and accent lighting that highlights a particular feature in the bathroom.

These three types of lighting can be used separately or in tandem, but all of them should be given some consideration, particularly in new construction or a major renovation, where you're not limited by existing wiring, fixtures, or switch locations.

Natural light also makes an important contribution. While there are obvious privacy issues with big windows in crowded neighborhoods, smaller windows set higher on the wall can provide ventilation as well as light. Bathrooms on the south, east, or west walls of the house may not need any artificial lighting during the day. And even bathrooms without exterior walls can get the benefits of natural light with a skylight or a solar tube, a roof-mounted skylight that pipes sunlight into the room via a reflective tube.

Hiring an interior designer or lighting specialist may be worth the expense when you have a generous budget and are working with a large, complex bathroom. But if that's not in the cards, visit a local lighting store for advice. Well-established retailers almost always have knowledgeable staff, and buying lighting fixtures from a locally owned business means the money stays in your community.

above right • Task lighting over the vanity, natural light from a window, and ambient lighting from a ceiling fixture (not shown) provide balanced lighting. Lights on either side of the mirror would cut shadows more effectively.

right • Natural light pouring into this bathroom from windows set high on the wall will get a boost from the large mirror over the vanity. It's supplemented by a fluorescent fixture above the mirror.

above · Placing lighting fixtures at eye level, one on each side of the mirror, will help reduce facial shadows.

left · This bathroom has a good mix of lighting: fixtures that flank the mirror over the vanity plus a dedicated fixture in the shower.

Because bathrooms are damp environments, special care should be taken to choose the right kinds of fixtures and to follow all code requirements. If you want a fixture in the shower, be certain it's rated for that use. If you plan on doing the wiring yourself, make sure you know what's required by code in your community and that you follow the script exactly. Better yet, hire a licensed electrical contractor to do the work.

above • Articulating lights over the vanity will create fewer harsh shadows than fixtures mounted directly on the wall.

above • A large window plus a mirror and two lights at the vanity make a bright, pleasant room with a good balance of natural and artificial light.

left • A pair of fixtures on each side of the mirror are set far enough from the wall to provide even light without shadows.

Lightbulbs

INCANDESCENT BULBS
$

- Inexpensive.
- Produce a pleasing, warm light.
- Don't last as long as several other types of lamps.
- Inefficient: more than 90 percent of the energy they use produces heat, not light.
- Efficiency requirements adopted by the government in 2007 will phase out many (but not all) standard incandescent bulbs between 2012 and 2014. There are already good alternatives on the market and more on the way.

FLUORESCENT LAMPS
$-$$

- Use less energy to produce the same amount of light as an incandescent bulb.
- Much longer lamp life.
- Compact fluorescent lamps (CFLs) screw into standard lamp bases.
- Some types can be dimmed, and lamps with a high color rendering index make people and objects look natural.
- Contain small amounts of mercury and should not be thrown away with household trash.
- Small-diameter fluorescent tubes can be hidden under cabinets or in ceiling coves to cast indirect light.

HALOGENS
$-$$

- New types of halogen bulbs, like the Halogená® bulbs from Philips, offer better energy efficiency than standard incandescent bulbs but not as much as CFLs or newer technology lamps.
- Halogens emit a bright, white light and look very similar to standard incandescent bulbs.
- Unlike CFLs, they reach their full lighting potential as soon as they are turned on, and they contain no mercury.
- They have high operating temperatures, very good color rendering, and last longer than incandescent bulbs.

- Low voltage halogens use transformers to step down 120-volt line current to 12 volts. The halogen bulbs used in low-voltage fixtures give off a white, crisp light, making them a good choice for accent lighting.
- Cable and monorail fixtures are stylish and contemporary, yet also can be expensive.

LEDS
$$-$$$

- Light-emitting diodes (LEDs) are becoming more widely available for residential use, but they're still somewhat of an expensive specialty item.
- White LEDs have a color rendering index equal to that of the best compact fluorescent lamps, according to the government's Energy Star program.
- Extremely long lamp life, up to 50,000 hours.
- More light output per watt than CFLs.

ESL TECHNOLOGY
$$

- Vu1 Corporation has developed another type of technology called "electron stimulated luminescence," lighting in which electrons cause phosphors in the lamp to generate light.
- Lamps produce the same quality of light as an incandescent and are dimmable and instant-on.
- Up to 70 percent more efficient than incandescents.
- Bulbs last five times as long as a standard incandescent bulb.
- Contain no mercury.
- Not widely available.

Creating Multiple Sources of Light

A key goal in the remodel of this California home was to add more light to a guest bathroom near the front entry, a job made all the more difficult by deep roof overhangs.

The design team (Studio Bergtraun Architects of Emeryville and Hart Wright Architects of San Francisco) started by rearranging an adjacent hallway and installing a large skylight. To borrow light from this source, the architects added a pair of narrow interior windows on the wall separating the bathroom from the hallway. And to balance this source of natural light, they installed daylight-temperature fluorescent bulbs in a light cove tucked behind the tub.

To connect different parts of the house visually, the architects used the same wall tile in all of the bathrooms as well as for the kitchen backsplash. Flooring flows seamlessly from the main parts of the house into the bathrooms. The guest bathroom's concrete vanity top also is a material that shows up elsewhere in the house.

Working on a tight budget, Studio Bergtraun/Hart Wright took on some of the construction themselves, including the cabinets built by Stuart Wright. The material, says Eliza Hart, "gives a uniquely warm and modern feel while relating it to the utilitarian sense of this period house, symbolic of 1950s modern design, like the Eichler homes and Eames furniture of the same era."

The bathroom vanity is wall-mounted, and most cabinets have drawers rather than doors for better functionality. Plumbing fixtures are "calm and modern," Hart says, "to blend in and visually disappear."

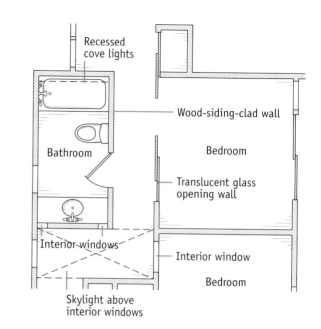

Recessed cove lights
Wood-siding-clad wall
Bathroom
Bedroom
Translucent glass opening wall
Interior windows
Interior window
Bedroom
Skylight above interior windows

Daylight-temperature fluorescent lamps tucked in a cove behind the tub supplement natural light from a pair of interior windows.

above • Plywood cabinets are symbolic of 1950s California modern design.

above left • A pair of windows in the wall between the bathroom and an adjacent hallway provide natural light.

left • Narrow bathroom windows don't open to the outside directly but borrow light from a skylight installed in a hallway on the other side of the wall.

Ambient Lighting

Ambient lighting doesn't have to be especially powerful or come from a high-end fixture to be effective. This type of lighting allows you to see what you're doing for general tasks—putting something in a linen closet, getting a glass of water, or hanging up fresh towels.

A simple ceiling fixture housing one or two CFLs should provide enough light for all but the largest bathrooms. Ceiling-mounted fan/light fixtures can be wired so the fan and light are switched independently, making this a cost-effective and low-tech way of providing ambient light.

With the right exposure, a window can provide all the ambient light you really need during the day, depending on the window's orientation. In new construction and extensive remodels, buy high-efficiency windows rated for the climate and the sun exposure. Check with your architect about an appropriate choice, or visit the Web site of the National Fenestration Rating Council (www.nfrc.org) for a thorough explanation of window characteristics.

Very small bathrooms may not need separate fixtures for ambient lighting and task or accent lighting. In a small powder room, for example, a pair of fixtures flanking a mirror over the sink may provide plenty of light for the whole room even if there's no overhead fixture.

Although an ambient light source can be simple, it doesn't have to be. In a large bathroom with a high ceiling, for instance, contemporary low-voltage lights on cables or an old-school chandelier might add style to the décor.

As to how much light to provide, the National Kitchen & Bath Association recommends round ceiling fixtures be at least 12 in. in diameter, with the bulb or bulbs rated at a total of 100 to 120 watts.

In a bathroom with multiple light switches in a single box, locating the switch for this all-purpose light in the position nearest the door will help you avoid fumbling for the switch in the middle of the night. Consider adding a dimmer switch for nighttime visits to the bathroom, when you're not looking for an intense blast of light, or buy an inexpensive night-light that turns itself off automatically during the day.

left • Thanks to a generously sized window, this vanity gets plenty of light even though the pendant fixtures are relatively small.

below • Recessed lighting fixtures over the vanity and tub provide unobtrusive task lighting. These fixtures, however, are potential energy and heat leaks when installed directly below an unconditioned space.

Task Lighting

Task lighting in a bathroom typically amounts to effective lighting around the vanity and mirror, and that usually means more than a single source of light.

The best approach is to install a light fixture on either side of the mirror at about eye level. This will cast light evenly on the face. Adding a light fixture over the mirror further reduces shadows, and choosing a light-colored countertop helps reflect light upward.

The worst lighting plan is just a single fixture directly over the vanity mirror. This will cast light downward, plunging eyes and parts of your face into shadow and making shaving or applying makeup difficult.

In new construction, planning ahead for a good lighting scheme is simple, but that's not always the case in a remodel. If the project includes a total gut, an electrician can add new lighting circuits and switches while the walls are open. If the remodel is less extensive, an electrician may still be able to snake new wires through the walls and tap into an existing circuit for power. The procedure is occasionally problematic, but by no means impossible.

Lights installed on each side of the mirror should have two 60-watt or two 75-watt bulbs (lower wattages, of course, for compact fluorescent lamps). If fluorescent-tube fixtures are the choice here, look for the highest CRI available: one 24-in., 20-watt tube on each side of the mirror, and two 24-in., 20-watt tubes over the mirror.

Lights in the shower are another kind of task lighting, and they make an excellent addition. Just remember the fixtures should be code approved for that location, meaning they should be vapor-proof fixtures. A separate shower fixture may be overkill in a small bathroom that already has an overhead light or in a shower with glass doors located near a window. But it's a real advantage in larger bathrooms

above • The enormous variety of fixtures on the market makes it possible to match lights with a particular architectural style or stylistic preference.

facing page, top • Mounting light fixtures directly over the mirror can create shadows on the face, but the bright walls here will help by reflecting some of the overhead light.

facing page, bottom • The soft paint color used around these vanity mirrors produces a cheerful glow.

with oversize showers, or when an opaque shower curtain is used. As with any other wiring changes, adding a shower fixture is a snap in new construction and somewhat more complicated in a remodel. If the shower has a tiled ceiling, for example, it may be more trouble than it's worth.

Bathrooms with large tubs also are good candidates for additional task lighting for the bathing area. Consider putting the lights on dimmers so the amount of light can match your mood.

These small opaque windows borrow light for the shower from an adjacent living area.

Adding Light without Sacrificing Privacy

Natural light is a great addition to a bathroom, but introducing it often means privacy issues. These four bathrooms prove that's not always the case. Windows can include frosted or textured glass, or be set high enough in the walls of a shower to eliminate privacy concerns. Glass block set into a shower stall can even draw light from an interior space, such as an adjacent hallway.

above • Opaque glazing in the windows over the tub guarantees privacy.

below • Installing a large window in the shower is an excellent way of providing strong ambient lighting, as long as you choose the right type of glass.

above • Setting windows in the shower high on the wall is one way of bringing in natural light without giving up privacy.

Accent Lighting

Accent lighting emphasizes a room feature, such as the texture or color of a wall, a cabinet, or the shape of a curved ceiling. Accent lighting is not essential from a practical point of view, but it can add a great deal to a room's appeal.

There are several types of accent lights. Pinhole or slot lights can be precisely adjusted to direct a very narrow beam of light toward an object—a shelf where glass jars of toiletries are displayed, for example. Wall washing or grazing is the use of lights to emphasize a textured surface, such as stucco, stone, or brick. Simple uplighting played on a painted wall can add mood to the room even when the wall doesn't have much texture.

Recessed low-voltage fixtures with halogen lamps cast a bright, sharply contrasting light without being obvious themselves. But accent lighting also can come in the form of low-profile fluorescent tubes set into shallow recesses beneath a mirror or even under a vanity.

As appealing as recessed lighting can be from a design standpoint, some of these fixtures have a potential energy drawback. In bathrooms located beneath an unconditioned attic or right below an insulated roof, recessed fixtures can let warm, moist air escape. At the least, this is a waste of energy, but air leaks also can contribute to condensation issues. To avoid these problems, make sure the fixtures are airtight and rated for contact with insulation. Otherwise, the fixture should be contained in a site-made, sealed enclosure that provides the clearance recommended by the manufacturer.

Accent lighting is one of those areas where expert advice, above and beyond what you'll get from your electrical contractor, can make a big difference.

If you have features in the bathroom you think warrant accent lighting, do your homework and talk to lighting professionals.

above • Light from fixtures installed beneath these cabinets floods the floor with light and reflects off the light-colored tile.

right • Lighting at the perimeter of this ceiling adds another dimension to the room.

Hidden cove lighting at the ceiling perimeter gently directs light upward.

Lighting Fixtures

Combining natural and artificial light from different types of fixtures makes any bathroom more attractive and more functional.

1. A large window in the shower makes the whole room bright and cheerful, and it's effectively balanced with both task and general lighting fixtures. 2. Three overhead lamps will cast a generous amount of light, although fixtures mounted on either side of the mirror would cast fewer shadows on the face. 3. Lamps concealed in the frame of the mirror will illuminate the face evenly, and in a small bathroom this concentrated task lighting may be all that's needed. 4. Pendant lights hanging over the tub create soft light when connected to a dimmer. 5. Light fixtures mounted directly to a large mirror over the sink provide even, balanced task lighting.

HEATING,

Mechanical systems do more than keep the room at a comfortable temperature and humidity.

COOLING &

They also control moisture to prevent damage in wall

Heating and cooling are more important in the bathroom than anywhere else in the house. First, you'll spend a lot of time in the bathroom without wearing a whole lot of clothing, so keeping the room comfortable is an obvious priority. Second, bathrooms are by nature humid environments. A properly sized mechanical system is essential to heading off potential problems caused by condensation.

Bathrooms are typically heated by the same system that serves other parts of the house. Especially in older homes, where heating equipment is antiquated or undersize, a bathroom can benefit from spot heat. There are a variety of options for supplemental heat, including underfloor electric heating mats, ceiling-mounted infrared lamps, and even electric or hydronic towel warmers. Some are more complicated than others to install (for more on the options, see p. 165).

Green building has helped focus attention on the importance of ventilation, not only to maintain healthy indoor air quality but also to prevent damage from condensation. As houses become more tightly sealed to lower heating and cooling costs, including effective ventilation should become a higher priority than it might have been in the past. At the very least, this means a quiet, good-quality fan that's vented to the outside.

More elaborate options, such as heat- or energy-recovery ventilators, help minimize the energy penalty of expelling warm air during the winter or bringing in hot, humid air during the summer. Installing timers or switches that turn on the fan automatically when humidity levels are high makes ventilation more predictable and effective.

Mechanical cooling isn't essential in all parts of the country, but it certainly makes life more bearable. In an older home, or in one with hydronic heat, central air-conditioning can be tough to add to a bathroom when the house doesn't already have air ducts. But a type of air-to-air heat pump called a "ductless mini-split" makes it possible to add cooling (and heating) to just a few rooms without conventional ducts. It's an option worth exploring in both new construction and renovations.

The volume of water used in large showers generates more moisture than opening even a nearby window can handle. Mechanical ventilation is a must.

left · An infrared light fixture in the ceiling near the shower provides spot radiant heating. Electric resistance heating installed beneath a tile floor is another way of taking the chill off the room without turning up central heat.

below · Properly sized ventilation equipment removes moisture that accumulates around showers and tubs. Capacity is based on the square footage of the room and the number of plumbing fixtures in the room.

Making Two Bathrooms from One

Portland, Maine, architects Anne Callender and her husband Joseph Delaney were living in a space-challenged home with a single full bathroom. When they mapped out a two-story addition to gain some extra space, they included this small but efficient master bath measuring just over 32 sq. ft.

To create space for the new master bath, the couple moved a wall and borrowed a few feet from the existing bathroom next door. They built a new wall in the master bedroom and tucked both a new shower and some closet space behind it.

A wall-mounted, tankless toilet helps save a few inches of floor space. The large sink is cantilevered out from the counter, another space-saving move. Behind the toilet is an 8-in.-deep cabinet that's 42 in. high and 48 in. wide, providing lots of storage for toiletries.

The cabinet under the sink is 14 in. deep with three doors, a perfect fit for towels, cleaning supplies, and additional toiletries.

Not including the shower, the bathroom measures just 60 in. by 77 in. with room for all the essentials and zero waste.

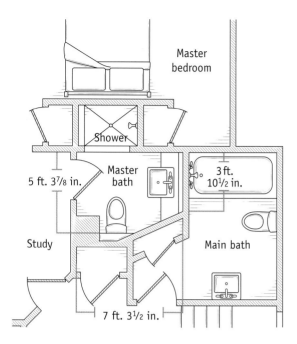

right • Unobtrusive but elegant detailing on the cabinet prevents the space from becoming too busy.

far right • The shower actually extends into a bump-out in the master bedroom. It's incorporated with two closets in a newly created space behind the bed.

left and above · A new master bath borrows space from an existing bath next door as well as the master bedroom, packing a lot into just over 32 sq. ft. A wall-mounted toilet and a cantilevered sink over a shallow vanity both help save floor space.

Fans

Elaborate ventilation systems that duct fresh air to every room in the house are becoming more common, but a relatively simple fan mounted in the ceiling and vented to the outside can still be an excellent hedge against moisture damage and mold as well as an effective way of maintaining good indoor air quality. Even better, a good-quality fan doesn't have to cost a fortune.

Fans are rated by how much noise they make, called "sones," and how much air they are capable of moving, expressed in cubic feet per minute, or CFM.

In a small bathroom, up to 100 sq. ft., industry guidelines suggest ventilation at the rate of 1 CFM per sq. ft. of floor area. In larger bathrooms, ventilation rates are based on the number and type of fixtures located in the bathroom (for more information, visit the Home Ventilating Institute's Web site at www.hvi.org). Fans located directly over the source of the moisture are most effective, so a larger bathroom with a separate tub and shower might have one fan over the shower and another over the tub.

The most basic bathroom fan incorporates both the fan and motor in a housing that's mounted in the ceiling. More powerful in-line fans can be located some distance away and serve more than one bathroom. However, they're more expensive and typically make more noise than a basic model.

One key to any fan installation: Never vent the fan to an attic, basement, or other conditioned space where moisture can condense on cold surfaces and lead to mold and decay. Make sure your builder runs the vent to the outside. Rigid pipe offers less resistance to airflow than corrugated plastic pipe.

Locating heating and cooling vents in the ceiling keeps them out of the way.

above • A large fan inlet combined with a light near the shower is effective in gathering moisture close to its source.

What to Look for in a Fan

Fan manufacturers use an odd metric for quantifying sound their products make. Noise levels are measured in "sones," units of perceived sound. The industry describes one sone as the amount of noise a quiet refrigerator makes in a quiet room.

Bargain fans, the kind that builders or electricians may install if you don't ask the right questions, may be rated at 4 or more sones. But at least two manufacturers—Panasonic and Broan—make fans rated at less than 1 sone, some as low as 0.3 sones. For practical purposes, these fans are inaudible while running.

If a fan is really noisy, chances are good you're less likely to use it, so it may not run as long as it should and consequently will be that much less effective. And fan noise is just plain irritating. Even though a large-capacity fan is going to make more noise than one designed for a very small bath, it pays to look for the lowest sone rating available for the fan size you need.

Bathroom Fans

CEILING-MOUNTED FANS
$

- Often packaged with a light, ceiling-mounted units include the fan and motor in a metal housing that is recessed into the ceiling.
- Some units draw air through a light fixture, with no visible grill.
- Look for a fan with a low sone rating for quiet operation.
- Some can be equipped with infrared light bulbs for spot heating.
- Small bathrooms need only one ceiling-mounted unit, but larger bathrooms with a number of separate fixtures may be better served with two.

WALL-MOUNTED FANS
$

- Good solution when framing or accessibility constraints prevent you from mounting a fan on the ceiling and venting through the roof.
- Ensure the unit has a screen to keep out critters.

IN-LINE FANS
$$

- Fans are installed in the duct itself, some distance away from the bathroom, and connected to one or more ceiling-mounted grills.
- Can draw air from more than one room; helpful for back-to-back bathrooms, for example, or multiple grills in a large bathroom with a number of fixtures.
- More powerful and more expensive than simple ceiling-mounted fans.
- Can be noisy.

CEILING-MOUNTED FANS

WALL-MOUNTED FAN

IN-LINE FAN

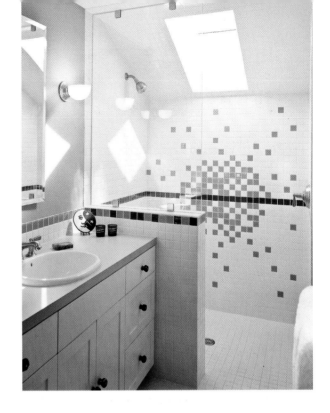

above • A centrally located fan may be enough to capture moisture generated at the tub, sink, and shower, but it must be sized with enough capacity.

above right • A large operable skylight over the shower can help vent moist air from the bathroom, but it's not a substitute for mechanical ventilation.

right • Perhaps the best place for a fan is right where the moisture starts—in this case, in the shower. A multiport in-line fan can be connected to multiple inlets, picking up moisture in the shower as well as from another point in the room.

SWITCHES AND TIMERS

Bathroom fans should continue to run for 20 minutes or so after a shower to completely clear the room of moisture, experts often recommend. While some homeowners are good about remembering that, many others aren't, and that's a good reason to consider installing a timer. Very simple models can be set easily to run for up to 30 minutes at the push of a button.

Programmable switches are a step up. They can be adjusted to turn on the fan for a certain amount of time every day, let's say between 7:00 and 7:20 a.m., for those folks who are on a rigid workday schedule and always shower at the same time. Programmable switches also can cycle a fan on and off throughout the day, which is useful when the bathroom fan is being used in lieu of a whole-house ventilation system. This is an option that should be discussed with a heating, ventilation, and air conditioning (HVAC) or energy professional since ventilation requirements vary with the size and construction of the house.

Another type of automatic switch is called a humidistat. It incorporates a humidity sensor and turns on the fan when moisture levels reach a certain threshold. When controlling airborne moisture levels, and not necessarily improving air quality, is the main objective, a humidistat is a hassle-free way of meeting your objective.

right · A simple fan/light mounted in the ceiling near the tub provides all the ventilation this small bath will need.

Ventilation Systems That Save Energy

In some ways it's counterintuitive to spend a lot of money heating or cooling your home and then running fans to blow all that conditioned air outside. Yet from an air-quality standpoint, it does make sense, and there are ways to minimize the energy penalty.

A heat recovery ventilator, or HRV, simultaneously draws fresh air into the house and pushes stale indoor air outside. The air streams pass through a heat exchanger so that some of the energy that would normally be lost is transferred to incoming air. For example, in winter, warm indoor air raises the temperature of incoming cold air from outside, lowering the amount of energy that's wasted. For an air-conditioned house in summer, the process would work in reverse.

Energy recovery ventilators, ERVs, are similar, but they also are capable of exchanging some of the moisture in the air stream.

When to choose an HRV over an ERV (or vice versa) is not a simple question, and even manufacturers may be dispensing incomplete advice. While climate is a key factor in choosing between the two, it's not the only criterion. Before making the decision, it would be best to read up on the subject in addition to talking with a competent HVAC installer. A good source of information on this and other indoor air-quality issues is GreenBuildingAdvisor (www.greenbuildingadvisor.com).

top left · A very simple timer has presets for running the fan from 10 minutes to an hour.

top right · More complex timers can be programmed to operate at certain times of day or even to switch on automatically when humidity levels reach a certain point.

above · If your fan is in good shape but too noisy, check the manufacturer's Web site to see if a retrofit kits is available for your model.

Heaters

There is one big advantage to installing an auxiliary heat source in the bathroom: you'll be comfortable even when the rest of the house is chilly.

Exactly what type of supplemental heat you choose will depend somewhat on what type of heating system you have for the rest of the house. If it's a hydronic system (that is, it runs on hot water), a toe-kick heater beneath a cabinet, a heated towel bar, or even a low-profile European-style radiator mounted on the wall are ways of getting additional heat.

Radiant-floor heat, which includes an underfloor network of plastic tubing for hot water, is another option that becomes possible during a major renovation when floors or ceilings are opened up. One advantage of radiant-floor heat is that there are no floor registers or radiators to get in the way; heat distribution is totally out of sight. But it's also an expensive option, and it can be complicated tying the tubing into an existing hot-water heating system.

Electric baseboard units on their own thermostats add heat, but the units themselves are often a headache in a smaller room, and they can rust. A better option is a grid of wires installed beneath a tile floor and connected to its own thermostat. Electric radiant heating systems, like those made by Nuheat, can be ordered both in stock and custom sizes and with one of a variety of thermostat options. There is even a grid designed for use in a shower. Electric radiant panels also are available for wall and ceiling installation.

Depending on local rates, any form of electric resistance heat can be expensive to operate. But electric heat also is very responsive.

A simple heat option is to buy a fan/light combination designed for an infrared bulb. Although it's low tech, standing under the light will keep you cozy.

above • Heated towel bars, which are available in both electric and hydronic versions, keep towels warm and can provide some space heating, too. Some models have enough capacity to heat the room.

below • A gas fireplace set at the foot of the tub and operated by a remote control is one way of providing spot heat—as long as there's enough space and the budget will permit.

top, middle, and bottom • Electric mats installed beneath the tile will keep floors warm and comfortable. They can be connected to their own thermostat.

Heaters

CEILING-MOUNTED HEAT LAMP
$

- Inexpensive and unobtrusive.
- Light fixture can be part of fan.
- Use with timer to limit run time.
- Heat from lamp not even.

TOE-KICK HEATER
$-$$

- Available in electric or hydronic models.
- Makes good use of wasted space beneath a cabinet.
- Fan distributes warm air.
- Depending on location of hot-water lines or electric cables, may be possible to add without major demolition.

WALL AND CEILING HEAT PANELS
$-$$

- Electric radiant panels available in a number of sizes that run on 120- or 240-volt current.
- Out of the way; don't take up floor space.
- Can be connected to a programmable thermostat to provide scheduled heat.
- Can be installed beneath ceiling drywall and kept completely out of sight.

ELECTRIC RADIANT FLOOR MAT
$-$$

- Grid of wires installed below finish floor, usually tile.
- Standard and custom sizes available.
- Available for wet locations, such as the shower.
- Out of sight; doesn't take up any floor area.
- Adds little floor height, so it's suitable for a remodel.

TOWEL WARMER/RADIATOR
$$

- Electric or hydronic models available.
- Depending on heating loads, can be used for supplemental heat or as sole source of bathroom heat.
- Keeps towels warm.
- Requires no floor space.

EUROPEAN-STYLE RADIATOR
$$$

- Low profile; takes up less space than conventional cast-iron radiator.
- Can be custom-made to curved shapes.
- Can replace conventional radiators without the need to overhaul existing hydronic heating system.

RADIANT FLOOR
$$$

- Installation requires removal of floor or access to bathroom floor from below.
- Requires hot water source, so not an option for hot-air distribution systems.
- Provides even, gentle heat.
- Takes up no floor area.

A 19th-Century Split Level

Wedging a new master bath into a three-story townhouse built in 1845 was complicated by an original floor plan that included staggered ceiling heights between the front and back of the house.

The floor in the existing master bath on the second floor at the rear of the house had previously been raised, giving the bath reduced headroom in addition to its 6-ft. width. Krieger + Associates Architects originally planned to remove the raised floor to increase the height of the ceiling, but it would still have been impossible to squeeze in the separate tub and shower plus a double-sink vanity the owners had requested.

The solution was to use the split-level effect as part of the design by lowering the floor and installing a new shower, tub, and toilet in the existing bathroom and turning the adjacent laundry room into a dressing room with a large, double-sink vanity. A pocket door divides the upper and lower areas.

When the old bath and its acoustical tile ceiling were torn out, the design team discovered "badly mutilated" ceiling joists, requiring new joists to be spliced in and plumbing and waste lines to be reconfigured.

To get more light into the lower part of the bathroom, Krieger added a taller window, using the existing header at the top of the window but cutting into the exterior brick to lower the sill.

The materials choices speak to the owners' traditional design sensibility with a simple, modern flair. They opted for hand-made blue and green ceramic tile for the shower, a vanity made from reclaimed wood stained a dark color, and a teak bench for the shower stall. The same reclaimed wood was used for the front of the tub, and the same tile used in the shower went into the backsplashes of the vanity sink and tub.

While the owners of the 19th-century townhouse appreciated the traditional spirit of the house, they also looked for ways to give it a modern flair.

above · The tub, toilet, and shower are located in the lower of two levels in this remodeled master bathroom. In the upper part are a two-sink vanity and dressing room. Handmade blue and green ceramic tile at the vanity complements the warm tones of the recycled wood in the cabinets.

right · The shower incorporates the same tile as the vanity, plus a teak bench.

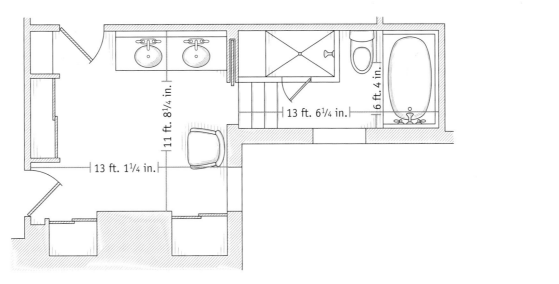

11 ft. 8¼ in.

13 ft. 6¼ in.

6 ft. 4 in.

13 ft. 1¼ in.

STORAGE

Bathrooms naturally attract clutter, but a combination of open shelving, built-ins,

freestanding cabinets, and the venerable medicine cabinet can keep things in order.

There is no single solution to the universal problem of where to store toiletries, towels, and other bathroom supplies. It's a good guess that a standard medicine cabinet over the sink won't offer nearly enough storage capacity for anything other than a powder room or guest bath.

So where does the rest of it go? Designers and manufacturers have come up with a number of solutions, including freestanding furniture, open shelving, and large built-in cabinets that use rollout hardware borrowed from kitchen applications. Some bathrooms may have enough countertop space to handle a lot of toiletries, reducing the need for cabinet storage. It's really a matter of personal preference.

An ideal arrangement includes a linen closet near the bathroom where towels, washcloths, and other bulky supplies can be stowed. If that's not possible, there are still plenty of options to consider.

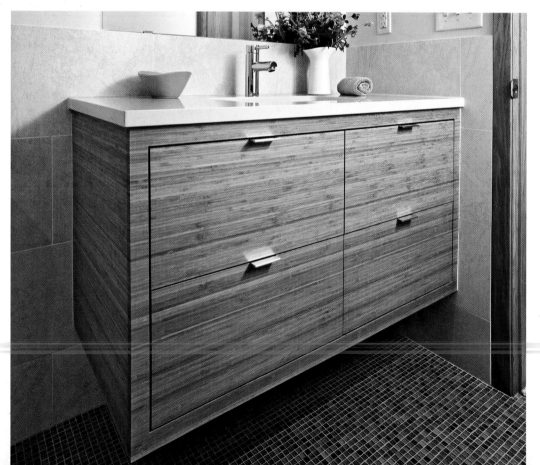

above • A large cabinet built into the wall provides ample storage for towels, soap, and other supplies.

left • Unlike traditional built-in cabinetry that rests on the floor, a wall-mounted unit looks less bulky and makes it easier to keep the floor clean.

facing page • Overhead cabinets are more often seen in the kitchen, but they can be just as successful in a bathroom.

Borrowing Ideas from the Kitchen

Kitchen cabinet manufacturers have introduced a variety of hinges, drawer slides, and other hardware to make kitchen storage more convenient, with an interesting ripple effect in the bathroom. For example, roll-out pantries that handle canned goods, spices, and other dry goods also can corral hair dryers and other small bathroom appliances, toothpaste, and toilet paper.

Large drawers on full-extension, ball-bearing slides are more convenient than deep, poorly lit cabinet shelves. While you lose some space side to side in the cabinet to the slides, chances are good you'll use more of the cabinet in the long run since you can more easily access the full space.

Because manufacturers often produce both bathroom and kitchen cabinet lines, it's worth seeing if some of the newer kitchen storage solutions are available for bathroom cabinetry. If you're ordering from a local cabinet shop, the hardware can be sourced from industry suppliers, such as Rev-A-Shelf. Many others just take a little bit of imagination and can be site-built from readily available materials and hardware.

Putting a large drawer on full-extension slides makes it easy to find what you're looking for. While full-extension slides often are standard on new cabinetry, slides are easy to retrofit on existing drawers.

above · In a kitchen, this kind of pullout would be used for canned goods or spices. It's just as successful in a bathroom.

left · A rollout wire basket becomes a convenient clothes hamper—easy to access yet just as quickly pushed out of sight.

Unifying Design with Light and Wood

There's an Asian flair to this bathroom in a renovated 1950s Minneapolis rambler, not only in the shoji paper wall sconces but also in the harmonic simplicity of materials and colors.

The bathroom is part of a bedroom suite in a new second floor. Architect David Wagner, a principal at SALA Architects, kept the palette of materials fairly simple, choosing to unify the design with the rich color of the Douglas fir in the ceiling, trim, and cabinets. Interior glass partitions visually link the bathroom and adjoining bedroom. Although the rooms are modestly sized, they don't feel that way.

Colors and textures were chosen carefully. "Cooler colors such as a light eucalyptus paint color, two tones of gray tile for the bathroom floor and shower, and a mottled blue-green for the sinks and countertop provide a counterpoint to the warm fir," Wagner says. These contrasting colors allow each of the materials to feel in harmony with the whole composition.

A cast concrete counter with integral sinks is a focal point of the new bathroom. The 8-in.-thick counter extends all the way across one wall, supported on one end by a fir cabinet and dropping down to become a seat in the shower on the other end of the room.

Wall-mounted faucets above the sinks extend from a Douglas fir backsplash, helping to keep the countertop open and uncluttered. At each side of the mirror are Japanese shoji paper wall sconces and wood-trimmed incandescent lighting.

A thick concrete vanity top, a focal point of this new bath in a remodeled home, stretches across the room and becomes a seat in the shower.

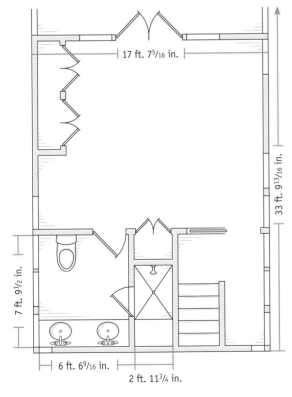

| 17 ft. 7⁵/₁₆ in. |
| 33 ft. 9¹³/₁₆ in. |
| 7 ft. 9½ in. |
| 6 ft. 6⁹/₁₆ in. |
| 2 ft. 11¾ in. |

above • Shoji wall sconces and spare trim details lend an Asian feel to the room.

above left • Architect David Wagner limited materials and colors and balanced the warm tones of the Douglas fir with cooler tile colors.

Cabinetry

Manufactured cabinetry comes in a tremendous range of styles, everything from Arts and Crafts and Shaker to modern minimalist. Beyond the cosmetic differences, what makes cabinets truly different is how they are made and what they are made from. Generally speaking, the more money you spend, the more durable the materials and the more careful the assembly. Cabinets fall into three broad categories: stock, semicustom, and custom.

above · This vanity combines drawers with open shelving, allowing towels and linens to become part of the room's décor.

left · Bathroom cabinetry doesn't have to be fancy. This simple cabinet with textured glass doors would be perfect in a smaller guest bath or powder room.

top • This freestanding cabinet tucked beneath a glass-topped vanity is an attractive and practical storage solution. Standard cabinet base units designed for solid countertops may need some extra work if you want a glass top.

above • Cabinets can help set the mood. This paneled vanity and marble vanity top are solidly traditional if not a little formal.

STOCK

Stock cabinets, the most economical on the market, are available in limited sizes, colors, and finishes. They're kept in stock at big-box stores and kitchen and furniture showrooms. While appealingly low in price, some stock cabinets are also low in quality. Stay away from cabinets made with thin, vinyl-covered particleboard. Look for tight joinery, drawers that open and close smoothly, and plywood rather than particleboard shelving and drawer bottoms.

SEMICUSTOM

The next grade up from stock is semicustom, and these cabinets offer more choices in finishes, hardware, and trim and molding details. Like stock cabinets, semicustom cabinets are made in 3-in. increments. Materials and hardware may be of higher quality (full-extension ball-bearing drawer slides, for example, rather than simple epoxy-coated slides and plywood construction over particleboard). You'll have to order the cabinets; lead times vary by manufacturer.

above • Restraint can be a virtue. This unadorned cabinet competes with neither the decorative tile on the floor nor the colorful subway tile in the shower.

right • When space permits, a large vanity that includes a lot of drawer space is ideal. Look for full-extension ball-bearing slides that travel easily.

above • Specialized cabinetry can fill awkward spaces. This round-front cabinet is ideal for a small powder room.

left • Against a neutral background in the rest of the room, the wood veneer on the face of this cabinet stands out sharply.

CUSTOM

Custom cabinets are at the top of the food chain, made completely to individual specifications and typically priced to match. This is the route to take if you want materials that large manufacturers typically don't offer, such as highly figured woods, special veneers, or unusual trim or finish details. Custom cabinets can be built to fit a space exactly, without the use of awkward filler strips, and you can pick precisely the construction techniques you prefer: dovetailed drawers and full mortise-and-tenon construction, for example.

Depending on what you order and who you're buying it from, lead times can be lengthy, possibly a matter of months, so that's something to ask about while shopping around. There are a few companies that specialize in custom cabinetry, but you might do just as well or better with a local cabinet shop or even an individual cabinetmaker in your area.

Though these industry labels for cabinetry are a helpful starting point, remember that it's not so much what they're called as how they're made that really counts. High-quality materials and finishes are very important for durability in the bathroom simply because of the potential for water damage. Avoid, if you can, particleboard, hardboard, and similar products unless they're specially engineered for water resistance. Avoid cabinets that come with drawers made from thin material stapled together at the corners.

above right • Bathroom furniture can reflect the overall architectural style of the house, in this case a strong Arts and Crafts theme.

right • Many furniture styles can be adapted to bathroom use. What looks like a Federal-style sideboard is really a marble-topped bathroom vanity.

left · Sleek and stylish, this vanity is well matched with the bathroom's overall décor and combines drawers with open shelving.

below · Given enough space, bathroom storage can include a dressing room with armoire-like closets, drawers, and even a shelf for a TV.

Cabinet Types

Although spending more usually buys better materials and finishes and more careful assembly, that's not always the case. Compare features, construction, and fit and finish carefully.

STOCK
$

- Most economical choice.
- Made in 3-in. increments.
- Limited number of cabinet styles and finishes.
- Kept in stock at big-box stores and kitchen and bath showrooms.
- Stock cabinetry can be a good buy, but check that materials are water resistant and robust enough for everyday use. Doors and drawers should operate smoothly.

SEMICUSTOM
$$

- More choices for finishes, materials, styles, wood types, and hardware.
- Manufactured in 3-in. increments.
- Can be ordered at home centers or kitchen and bath showrooms. Lead times for delivery vary by manufacturer.
- Materials and construction techniques typically are of higher quality than stock cabinets. Look for dovetailed drawers, full-extension drawer slides, sturdy plywood cabinet boxes, and hardwood drawer sides and face frames.
- When ordering cabinets through a kitchen/bath showroom, ask whether their services include a personal visit by a designer to ensure cabinets are correctly sized and installed properly.

CUSTOM
$$$

- Can be built to a specific height, width, and depth.
- Materials and construction techniques typically are of the best quality.
- You can specify wood species, trim details, and hardware, including door and drawer pulls, hinge type, and specific molding profiles.
- Custom finishes and paint colors available.
- Lead times can be quite long.
- Available from manufacturers that specialize in custom cabinetry, such as Rutt, and ordered through local retailers. Shopping locally or regionally also is an attractive option. Check with smaller cabinet shops, local companies, and individual cabinetmakers.
- Custom makers offer highly personalized design services.

above • Instead of conventional drawers, this custom installation uses wicker baskets on open shelves for storage. The layout also provides generous countertop space.

above • Although this wall-mounted vanity doesn't offer a huge amount of storage, it's a good fit with the minimalist setting.

right • Simple and effective, this two-level built-in combines undersink storage with an adjacent full-height cabinet.

WALL-MOUNTED AND FREESTANDING CABINETS

Built-in cabinets with a toe-kick at the base have long been a traditional choice for bathrooms as well as kitchens, but freestanding cabinets that look more like furniture (see pp. 186–187) and wall-mounted cabinets are two other options worth exploring.

If you have a favorite piece of furniture, it might find a new home in the bathroom; an antique chest of drawers or a side table, for example, might easily fit in a corner and be used to store toiletries. Larger pieces can be adapted for use as a vanity, providing the materials and construction are robust enough for use in this environment.

Because its full weight is supported by framing inside the wall, a wall-mounted vanity requires more careful planning so blocking and structural wall framing can be located correctly. A wall-hung cabinet may not have quite as much storage capacity as a built-in, but it simplifies cleaning because there are no obstructions for a vacuum or mop. Wall-mounted cabinets have a light, airy look that can help small spaces seem larger than they are.

Another consideration is cabinet height. While built-in vanities can be ordered in a range of standard heights, sometimes they're just too low for taller adults. Switching to a wall-mounted cabinet allows installation at whatever height is most comfortable for you, not an arbitrary height dictated by convention or a cabinet manufacturer.

above • A simple freestanding cabinet combining drawers, undersink storage, and open shelves is a good match with the rustic décor of this bathroom.

right • A custom installation can include unique details, such as this dressing table created with a countertop stretching across two base cabinets.

above • Installing cabinets of different depths and heights is another way of adding vitality to bathroom storage. Here, lots of shadow lines and details make the room lively and interesting.

left • Custom cabinets can be built to match other trim details in the room, an extra step but one that makes the setting a cohesive whole.

Stand-Alone Furnishings

Moving a piece of furniture into the bathroom and adapting it for use as a vanity or using it as is for storage can be a great way of making the bathroom seem homey and comfortable.

Any good cabinet shop can check to see whether the necessary internal adjustments can be made to a particular piece of furniture. Modifying a chest of drawers into a vanity, for example, could require the removal of some internal drawer dividers or frames—not possible with every piece, but an

option that may be worth exploring. If you already own the piece, modifying it is probably going to be less expensive than buying new.

Manufactured bathroom furnishings that look like freestanding tables also are available, or you can turn to a local cabinetmaker and commission a simple piece in your choice of wood and finish. Although storage in open-framed tables is limited, the style can be an appealing alternative to boxy built-ins.

1. A black-lacquered table reflects the Chinese theme of this bathroom while acting as a backdrop for some of the homeowner's Chinese art. 2. A simple metal side table tucks comfortably into a corner and offers plenty of storage for a guest bath. The flat finish blends well with the rest of the room. 3. A simple stand uses baskets instead of drawers for storage. The open design keeps it from looking clunky. 4. This attractive vanity combines open shelving with two deep drawers and manages to look like a traditional piece of furniture.

A Design That's All about the Details

One of the chief design goals in the master bathroom renovation at this Minneapolis house was to include the exuberant detailing appropriate for its Victorian heritage while keeping the room calm and understated at the same time.

Working with the same footprint as the original bathroom, Rehkamp Larson Architects kept the range of materials to a minimum, combining custom metal work and cabinetry with a simple palette of finishes. This was part of the design team's philosophy—to highlight the details of the space and address functional needs in a beautiful way.

The wall tile, vanity top, and tub deck all are Calcutta marble. The light tones of the cabinetry and walls are a good match with the stone. The darker beams and window trim help connect the new bathroom with woodwork in the rest of the house as well as the oiled bronze fixtures and hardware in the bathroom. These darker elements help draw the eye up and around the room.

A feeling of openness throughout the room was important to the homeowners, and the custom metal and glass shower contributes to the effect. The dark bronze frame and frosted glass are meant to be reminiscent of an English garden conservatory.

Cabinetry was designed with attention to proportions, color, and texture. The open shelves and furniturelike legs of the vanity help prevent it from feeling heavy or boxy. To reduce visible clutter, an open alcove on one side of the makeup vanity can accommodate necessary appliances and toiletries. Decorative metal grilles above the vanity area conceal in-wall speakers.

right • **This refurbished master bath incorporates a custom metal and glass shower surround instead of more conventional solid walls to keep the room feeling spacious.**

above • **The vanity design makes it look more like furniture and less boxy than a typical built-in.**

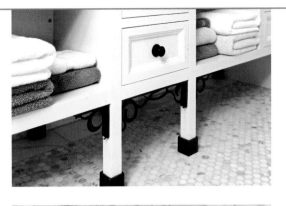

top and above · Designers drew on the Victorian heritage of the house in such details as the bathtub and vanity faucets and bronze feet for the vanity.

above · Working with the room's original footprint, designers were able to work in a large tub as well as a large shower.

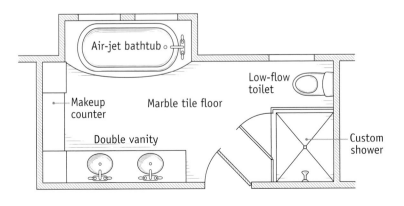

Air-jet bathtub

Makeup counter

Marble tile floor

Low-flow toilet

Double vanity

Custom shower

above · A built-in dressing table includes nooks for towels and cabinets below for additional storage.

Medicine Cabinets

A medicine cabinet is probably the simplest way to expand storage in the bathroom. Whether surface mounted or built into the wall between studs, a medicine cabinet is tailor-made for all the odds and ends that collect around the sink. It's also a practical necessity for a bathroom with a pedestal sink, which offers very little room for toiletries on its own.

If your bathroom doesn't have a medicine cabinet, adding one should be relatively simple, especially if you choose a surface-mounted design. Installing a recessed cabinet isn't an overwhelming job, either, provided plumbing and wiring runs inside the wall won't interfere. Manufactured cabinets are sized to fit standard wall framing.

Built-in cabinets don't intrude into the room, and they can be custom-made to virtually any size and shape as long as the builder knows in advance what you want. Wall framing is typically 16 in. on center, but it can easily be adjusted for a wider cabinet as the room is being framed. Trim surrounding the cabinet can be elaborate, or it can disappear altogether in favor of an unadorned mirror, making this kind of installation very flexible.

If you're looking for something a little funky or a cabinet to match a period home, a variety of online sources offer vintage medicine chests. Or check local secondhand shops, flea markets, and antique stores.

above • Medicine cabinets don't have to be located over the sink. This small, flush-mount cabinet works just as well to the side, saving the over-the-sink spot for a larger mirror.

left • A traditional surface-mounted medicine cabinet over the sink is a good choice when a small countertop or pedestal sink offers little room for storage.

above • Combined with small open shelves, the frameless mirrored doors don't interfere with other elements in the room.

above right • Large mirrored doors without frames or pulls look clean and uncluttered.

right • Recessed cabinets flanking a large central mirror offer his-and-hers storage options.

Open Shelves and Cubbies

The open-shelf look can range anywhere from elegant to campy. Open shelving can make a bathroom feel more spacious, but don't forget that whatever you are storing is out in the open for all to see. While showing off bottles of mouthwash and half-used tubes of toothpaste might not interest you, displaying special soaps, bath salts, and even cotton balls and the like in glass containers can add to the room's decor and put them within reach. Of course, towels, washcloths, and other linens are prime candidates for this kind of storage as well.

1. There's nothing sloppy about this open-shelf unit at the foot of the tub. Choosing what to put out in the open is key. **2.** A custom built-in combines open shelves, enclosed cabinets, and a drawer beneath a seat. Construction is extremely simple. **3.** An open storage area gets towels within convenient distance of the tub, and it makes a more interesting detail than a blank wall. **4.** A sliding door on an overhead track opens to reveal a full array of bathroom supplies on simple, slatted shelving. The arrangement is a perfect match with the room's relaxed décor. **5.** Shelves made from tempered glass are less overwhelming visually than solid shelving. **6.** Shelves built into the wall display towels, washcloths, and a few simple containers. Aligning the top shelf with the top of the beadboard wainscoting helps the cabinet blend into the room.

FINISHING

Paint, wallpaper, window coverings, and other final touches are the details that pull the room together, completing the project and giving it a character all its own.

TOUCHES

The hard work is done: mechanical systems and fixtures installed, lights updated, wiring and plumbing in. Yet the room really won't be complete without a few important finishing touches. Paint, wallpaper, window treatments, decorative art, and even the texture and color of bath towels all can contribute to the overall success of a new or refurbished bathroom.

Compared to the challenging and time-consuming work that goes into the underlying structure of a bathroom, these enhancements will be the most economical part of the project. Low-cost, however, doesn't mean low-impact. Even seemingly small moves can add appreciably to the overall impact the room makes and its thematic connection to the rest of the house.

The tools at your disposal can be pretty simple: paint and wallpaper, decorative art that can be hung on the walls, small splashes of color from potted plants, towels, soap, and toiletries. With more planning, and a greater investment, you can branch into more elaborate surface decorations, such as *trompe l'oeil* painting and murals. But start small and see what happens.

above • Against a palette of subdued colors, the bright tile in the back of the tub, the potted plant on the vanity top, and even a bar of soap become colorful focal points.

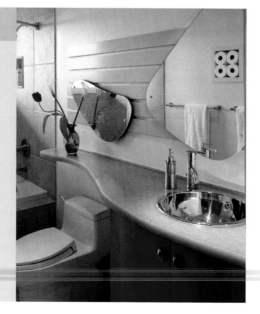

Adding Curves

Bathrooms tend to have a rectilinear character. The room itself is almost always rectangular, with a rectangular tub and shower stall and boxy cabinets. Adding a curved section of countertop or an organically shaped mirror or wall decoration can be an effective way of enlivening the room. In this bathroom, both color and shape have been used to make the vanity and wall behind it the focal point of an otherwise plain room.

above · Against a background of pale green paint, a bright yellow flower is a simple yet eye-catching detail.

above left · A combination of patterned wallpaper and a colorful window covering gives this bathroom an unmistakable period flavor.

left · Matching the color of the walls to decorative tile in the wainscoting is a powerful way of pulling the room together visually.

Paint

Paint is an extremely simple way of adding or removing color, and both of these objectives can be important. In a bathroom where tile wainscoting, a textured stone floor, or an elaborate tub surround is the focal point, vivid wall colors may not work as well as quiet ones simply because too many colors and textures competing for attention can be unsettling. Conversely, in a bathroom where plumbing fixtures, tile, and other features are on the bland side, a wall or two of vivid color can make the room a lot more interesting.

What makes some colors pleasing and others alarming or off-putting is, of course, a matter of personal preference. But because bathrooms are often where women apply makeup, some designers suggest avoiding colors that make skin tones look unnatural or unhealthy. Color can play a role in mood; some are calming, others are stimulating (bathtub manufacturers, in fact, rely on the soothing effects of color to promote bathtub lighting systems; see p. 80).

Because paint color is so easy to change and bathrooms are rarely huge spaces, why not experiment? If one color or color combination doesn't have the impact you're looking for, the bathroom can always be repainted with a minimal investment of time and dollars. Just remember that cost usually affects quality: Buy the best paint you can get your hands on.

left · Bright colors that might seem overwhelming elsewhere make this child's bath fun and cheerful.

right · Coordinating colors on the walls, cabinetry, and window treatment give this bath a pleasing cohesion, and the mellow colors are soothing.

facing page · White cabinetry, mirrors, and wainscoting help the deep blue walls stand out while minimizing the room-shrinking quality that a dark paint can have.

PAINT

LATEX

- Dries quickly.
- Cleans up with water.
- Buy high-quality paint made with acrylic latex.
- Contains very small amounts—or no—volatile organic compounds (VOCs). No-VOC formulations are favored by green-building advocates to maintain indoor air quality.
- Working characteristics have improved dramatically in recent years. Water-based paints are now a focus of research and development by manufacturers as use of oil paints declines.

OIL

- Some painters still prefer oil-based paint for trim because it flows out smoothly and dries hard.
- Becoming harder to find as government regulations clamp down on VOCs that oil-based paints contain.

- Cleans up with solvents.
- Odor from curing paint may last for days and may adversely affect those with chemical sensitivities.
- Avoided by green-building advocates because of VOCs.

SHEEN

- Sheen is a measure of how reflective the cured paint film is, ranging from flat (no sheen) to gloss (high sheen).
- Where surfaces are going to be scrubbed periodically or are subjected to more wear and tear, higher sheens are typically used because the paint film is more durable.
- Some flat paints are advertised as durable enough for vigorous washing.
- Surface flaws are more easily visible under a coat of high-gloss paint; flat paint minimizes defects.

Bath with a View

This master bathroom, part of a new addition and renovation at a 1908 Minneapolis home, makes the most of panoramic views of a terraced backyard garden and, in the distance, Lake Harriet.

Rehkamp Larson Architects restored and reused metal-framed windows, helping to blend the bathroom with the rest of the century-old house. Pedestal sinks, a claw-foot bathtub, and an antique crystal light fixture also help give the bathroom a vintage flavor.

"While the vaulted hall and bath ceilings might be considered a modern element, the dark chocolate paint color keeps the spatial drama in check," architect Jean Rehkamp Larson says of the re-designed room.

Careful detailing, particularly in the tile work, also is important. A tiled carpetlike pattern in the floor of the hall leading to the main part of the bath and a double row of mosaics near the top of the tile wainscoting reinforce the unusual color of the upper walls and ceiling.

The white floor, white trim and fixtures, and storage closet all help balance the darker upper part of the room. Although the range of colors is strictly limited, the room makes a striking visual impact.

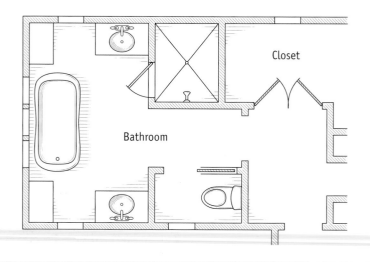

facing page • White tile wainscoting, a light-colored tile floor, and white trim balance the unusual chocolate-colored upper walls. A band of tile near the top of the wainscoting connects the two.

right • A carpetlike pattern of tile in the hallway leading to this master bath is typical of the attention to detail that makes the space a success.

below • The bathroom benefits from distant views of Lake Harriet in Minneapolis. The metal-framed windows are refurbished.

Wallpaper

Wallpaper has seen ups and downs in popularity in the years since 19th-century manufacturing brought the price within reach of the middle class. It's available in an enormous variety of colors, patterns, and price ranges and in many of its forms has the potential to add two elements that most painted surfaces lack: pattern and texture.

There are brightly colored prints and offbeat borders that can jazz up a child's bath or a bathroom in a summer cottage: sea creatures, surfboards, and tropical fruit. You'll find full-wall murals featuring Tuscan villas or palm trees leaning over a tropical beach.

One of the best uses for wallpaper is in decorating period homes, which would have had wallpaper when originally built. Wallpaper patterns varied in complexity and style depending not only on the era in which it was originally made but also in the socio-economic rank of the homeowners and the architectural style of their home. If you're trying to restore a correct period style in an older home, enlisting the help of a local wallpaper pro would be time well spent. The many online sources of information also are very helpful.

Always make sure the wallpaper you choose is appropriate for use in a bathroom, where high humidity, occasional exposure to water, and wear and tear are to be expected. Natural grass and bamboo reed wallpapers, for example, may look great in the living room or bedroom but would be impractical choices in a bath.

The color of this wallpaper isn't overwhelming, but it has a ribbed texture that gives the walls discernible depth.

above · Wallpaper can be part of a carefully orchestrated color scheme, as evidenced in this bathroom.

above left · Wallpaper doesn't have to be dowdy or old-fashioned. This bright wall covering of undersea creatures, is ideal for a child's bath.

left · The elegant pattern of this paper complements the antique dressing table mirror, chair, and other period details in the room.

Window Coverings

Window coverings in a bathroom are primarily there for privacy. That much is obvious. But there are a variety of ways to accomplish that, from louvered wood shutters and full-length shades to curtains that cover only the lower portion of windows around the tub or shower. Window coverings should match the style of the room: basic white half-curtains look in keeping in a farmhouse bathroom, heavily brocaded swag curtains with a set of inner curtains in a Victorian bath.

Curtains also become design elements, picking up colors used elsewhere in the room or introducing a decorative motif compatible with other features or decorations. Curtains and shades also are useful for controlling strong sunlight in western-facing windows, helping to keep interiors cool in summer. In bathrooms with large windows, thermal curtains reduce winter heat losses significantly.

Louvered shutters are an alternative to fabric curtains. They can be adjusted for light and privacy as needed and swung open completely when they're not needed. Shutters offer excellent ventilation, a plus in places where summers are hot.

above • These windows are set high enough in the wall that they are not a privacy concern, so window treatments can be purely decorative.

right • The combination of louvered shutters with roll-down window treatment means more color—and privacy—can be added at a moment's notice.

above • Shades cover only the bottom half of the windows around the tub, providing privacy where it counts but still admitting light.

far left • Louvered interior shutters block sight but allow good natural ventilation.

left • Sometimes the window treatment is the window itself. Substituting glass block for a conventional window unit means lots of light and lots of privacy.

Connecting Spaces with Light and Air

Wooded surroundings of this home in Upper Saddle River, New Jersey, set the tone for a master bathroom remodel. A 10-ft.-long bank of windows makes the most of a lush outdoor setting, while the vaulted ceiling helps the bathroom feel open and airy.

The shower, measuring roughly 4 ft. by 6 ft., is separated from the rest of the room by half walls rather than a full enclosure, a functional detail that keeps water contained but also makes the shower part of the room as a whole.

Holly Rickert of architects Ulrich, Inc., specified Italian ceramic tile in shades of blue, gray, and green, meant to harmonize with colors found in nature. Five different sizes and shapes of the same porcelain variety were used, including shards for the shower and one of the two vanity tops. As a result, surfaces relate well to each other without being identical.

Copper also helps unify the design. It's used at the round mirror over one of the vanities, in planters that sit on top of the half-height shower walls, and as a waterfall detail inside the shower.

A black-lacquer finish, rattan cabinetry, and the warm tones of wood were designed to create a soft look and lend an Asian feel the homeowners liked.

Instead of a conventional door entry, the bathroom uses a panel of etched glass to define the space. Rickert says the panel depicts a classic Japanese woodcut of Mount Fuji.

Copper becomes a unifying material. It's used in the mirror over the vanity, in a shower detail, and in planters on top of half walls around the shower.

above · Half-height partitions divide this New Jersey bathroom into functional spaces without closing anything off. A large bank of windows and a vaulted ceiling keep the room airy.

left · An etched glass panel helps separate the bathroom from the adjoining bedroom. Without a conventional door, the spaces flow together.

Details That Make a Difference

As with any room in the house, add personal details to your bathroom to help make it feel special, create a theme, or unify a color scheme. Be mindful of any artwork, though, as moisture levels will obviously be higher in the bath than in any other room in the house, and this can potentially ruin the work. Shower curtains, throw rugs, and accessories can be used to complete the space.

1. Simple decorative touches, like these starfish propped on top of the wainscoting and seashells in the built-in, can reflect a special interest of the homeowner or connect the room to its locale. **2.** Framed prints add color, and they're easy to change periodically to give the room a fresh look. **3.** A splash of color that contrasts sharply with the background can be an effective detail. **4.** Monogrammed towels on display beneath an antique vanity spell homey tradition. **5.** The artwork over the tub takes center stage and is the inspiration for the bath's color scheme.

RESOURCES

Organizations and Associations

THE AMERICAN INSTITUTE OF ARCHITECTS
www.aia.org
(800) AIA-3837

BATHTUB REFINISHING ASSOCIATION OF AMERICA
www.braoa.org
(310) 893-0847

CENTER FOR UNIVERSAL DESIGN
www.design.ncsu.edu/cud
(919) 515-3082

GREEN BUILDING ADVISOR
www.greenbuildingadvisor.com
(866) 325-2558

MARBLE INSTITUTE OF AMERICA
www.marble-institute.com
(440) 250-9222

NATIONAL ASSOCIATION OF HOME BUILDERS
www.nahb.org
(800) 368-5242

NATIONAL ASSOCIATION OF THE REMODELING INDUSTRY
www.nari.org
(847) 298-9200

NATIONAL KITCHEN & BATH ASSOCIATION
www.nkba.org
(800) 843-6522

TILE COUNCIL OF NORTH AMERICA
www.tileusa.com
(864) 646-8453

Manufacturers and Suppliers

ADAGIO
www.adagiosinks.com
(877) 988-2297
Sinks

AMERICAN STANDARD
www.americanstandard-us.com
(800) 442-1902
Plumbing fixtures

ARMSTRONG
www.armstrong.com
(800) 233-3823
Flooring

BROAN-NUTONE
www.broan-nutone.com
(800) 445-6057
Ventilation equipment

CHICAGO FAUCETS
www.chicagofaucets.com
(847) 803-5000
Faucets

DELTA FAUCET CO.
www.deltafaucet.com
(800) 345-3358
Faucets

ELJER MANUFACTURING CO.
www.eljer.com
(800) 442-1902
Plumbing fixtures

ELLA'S WALK-IN TUBS
www.ellaswalkintubs.com
(800) 480-6850
Walk-in bathtubs

FANTECH
www.fantech.net
(800) 747-1762
Ventilation equipment

GROHE FAUCETS
www.groheamerica.com
(630) 582-7711
Faucets

JACUZZI WHIRLPOOL BATH
www.jacuzzi.com
(800) 288-4402
Whirlpool bathtubs

KEIDEL SUPPLY CO.
www.keidel.com
(513) 351-1600
Fixtures and faucets

KOHLER CO.
www.kohler.com
(800) 456-4537
Plumbing fixtures

MANSFIELD PLUMBING PRODUCTS
www.mansfieldplumbing.com
(877) 850-3060
Plumbing fixtures

MTI WHIRLPOOLS
www.mtiwhirlpools.com
(800) 783-8827
Whirlpool bathtubs

MYSON INC.
www.mysoninc.com
(800) 698-9690
Towel warmers

PANASONIC
www.panasonic.com
(866) 292-7292
Ventilation equipment

PORCHER
www.porcher-us.com
(800) 359-3261
Plumbing fixtures

RUNTAL NORTH AMERICAN
www.runtalnorthamerica.com
(800) 526-2621
Heated towel bars

SANIFLO INC.
www.saniflo.com
(800) 363-5874
Macerating toilets

TOTO
www.totousa.com
(770) 282-8686
Plumbing fixtures

VICTORIA + ALBERT
www.englishtubs.com
(800) 421-7189
Soaking tubs

CREDITS

CHAPTER 1

p. 6: © Karen Melvin

p. 8: © Gridley + Graves, architect: Moulton Layne, P.L., www. moultonlayne.com (top); © Gridley + Graves, architect: Moulton Layne, P.L., www.moultonlayne. com; interior designer: Rod Mickley Interiors, www.rodmickley.com (bottom)

p. 9: © Randy O'Rourke

p. 10: © Olson Photographic (top); © Mark Lohman (bottom)

p. 11: © Mark Lohman

p. 12: © Ken Gutmaker (top); © Anne Gummerson (bottom)

p. 13: © Tria Giovan

pp. 14-15: © Ken Gutmaker (all)

p. 16: © Olson Photographic

p. 17: © Eric Roth

p. 19: © Greg Hursley (left); © Todd Caverly (right)

p. 20: © Mark Lohman

p. 21: © Ken Gutmaker (left); © Greg Hursley (right)

p. 23: courtesy Kohler

p. 24: © Mark Lohman, design: Nicholas/Budd Architects (left); © Olson Photographic (right)

p. 26: © Ken Gutmaker (top); courtesy Kohler (bottom)

p. 27: courtesy Kohler

pp. 28-29: © Trent Bell

p. 30: © Karen Melvin, design: Carla Bast Interior Design, M.E. Gardiner Interior Design

p. 31: © Ken Gutmaker

CHAPTER 2

p. 32: © Eric Roth

p. 34: © Karen Melvin, design: David Heide Design

p. 35: © Mark Lohman (top left); courtesy Kohler (top right); © Mark Lohman, design: Nancy McDonald Design (bottom)

p. 36: © Mark Lohman

p. 37: courtesy Kohler (top and bottom left); © Gridley + Graves (bottom right)

p. 38: © Mark Lohman

p. 39: © Tria Giovan (top left); courtesy Kohler (top right); © Eric Roth (bottom right)

p. 40: courtesy Kohler (top); © Mark Lohman, design: Rohl Kitchen & Bath (bottom left); © Eric Roth (bottom right)

p. 41: © Mark Lohman, design: Barclay Butera Inc.

p. 42: © Art Grice (left); © Mark Lohman (right)

p. 43: courtesy Kohler (top and bottom)

p. 44: © Tria Giovan (top); courtesy Kohler (bottom left and bottom right)

p. 45: © Mark Lohman, design: Kathryn Designs

p. 46: © Todd Caverly (top); © Mark Lohman (bottom)

p. 47: © Eric Roth (top left); © Dulcie Horowitz (top right); © Todd Caverly (bottom)

p. 48: © Tria Giovan

p. 49: © Ken Gutmaker (top); © Tria Giovan (bottom)

p. 51: © Olson Photographic (top left and bottom); © Ken Gutmaker (top right)

pp. 52-53: © Zach DeSart (all)

p. 54: courtesy American Standard

p. 55: courtesy Kohler (top left); courtesy American Standard (bottom left and right)

p. 56: © Eric Roth (all)

p. 57: © Eric Roth

p. 58: © Gridley + Graves, architect: Moulton Layne, P.L., www. moultonlayne.com; interior designer: Rod Mickley Interiors, www.rodmickley.com (top right); © Gridley + Graves, design: SCW Interiors, www.scwinteriors.com (bottom right); © Eric Roth (left)

p. 59: © Ken Gutmaker (left); © Mark Lohman, design: Janet Lohman Interior Design (right)

p. 60: courtesy Kohler (top); © Ken Gutmaker (bottom)

p. 61: courtesy Kohler (top left and bottom left); courtesy American Standard (bottom right)

p. 62: © Mark Lohman, design: Janet Lohman Interior Design (top); courtesy Mansfield EcoQuantum (bottom)

p. 63: © Eric Roth

p. 64: courtesy American Standard

p. 65: courtesy American Standard (all)

p. 66: courtesy Toto USA (top); courtesy Kohler (bottom)

p. 67: courtesy Villeroy & Boch (top left); courtesy Kohler (top right); courtesy Duravit (bottom)

pp. 68-69: © Greg Auseth (all)

CHAPTER 3

p. 70: © Mark Lohman, design: Carolyn Oliver Design

p. 72: © Mark Lohman, design: Michael Lee Architects (right); © Karen Melvin, design: Sawhill Kitchens (left)

p. 73: © Eric Roth (top); © Ken Gutmaker (bottom)

p. 74: © Eric Roth

p. 75: © Eric Roth (top); © Karen Melvin, design: Beret Evenstad Design, Martha O'Hara Interiors (bottom)

p. 76: © Mark Lohman, design: Michael Lee Architects (top); © Eric Roth (bottom)

p. 77: © Randy O'Rourke

p. 78: © Karen Melvin, design: Pappas Design

p. 79: © Tria Giovan (top); © Karen Melvin, design: Touraine Richmond Architects (bottom)

p. 80: courtesy Kohler (top); courtesy Meditub (bottom)

p. 81: © Mark Lohman (left); © Tria Giovan (right)

p. 82: © Eric Roth

p. 83: © Mark Lohman

p. 84: © Mark Lohman, design: Cynthia Marks Interiors

p. 85: © Karen Melvin, design: Calibur Legacy Builders

pp. 86-87: Ken Gutmaker (all)

p. 88: © Ken Gutmaker (top and bottom)

p. 89: © Ken Gutmaker

p. 90: © Ken Gutmaker

p. 91: © Karen Melvin, design: Merillat Cabinetry (top); © Tria Giovan (bottom)

p. 92: © Eric Roth (top); Ken Gutmaker (bottom left); © Mark Lohman, design: Janet Lohman Interior Design (bottom right)

p. 93: © Ken Gutmaker

p. 94: © Mark Lohman (top); © Karen Melvin, design: Casa Verde (center); © Mark Lohman, design: Nancy McDonald Design (bottom)

p. 95: © Ken Gutmaker (top left); © Mark Lohman (bottom left and right)

p. 96: © Eric Roth

p. 97: © Mark Lohman (all), design: Rohl Kitchen & Bath (top left and bottom right), design: Kathryn Designs (top right)

pp. 98-99: © Zach DeSart (all)

CHAPTER 4

p. 100: © Eric Roth

p. 102: © Olson Photographic (top); © Tria Giovan (bottom left); © Ken Gutmaker (bottom right)

p. 103: © Tria Giovan

p. 104: © Eric Roth (bottom left); courtesy *Fine Homebuilding* magazine, © The Taunton Press, Inc. (right)

p. 105: courtesy *Fine Homebuilding* magazine, © The Taunton Press, Inc. (all)

p. 106: © Olson Photographic (top); © Gridley + Graves, design: SCW Interiors, www.scwinteriors.

com (bottom); courtesy Sharon McCormick Design (right)

p. 107: © Randy O'Rourke

p. 108: © Eric Roth (top); © Mark Lohman, design: Janet Lohman Interior Design (bottom)

p. 109: © Michael Fein (left); © Eric Roth (right)

pp. 110-111: © Trent Bell (all)

p. 112: © Ken Gutmaker (top); © Randy O'Rourke (bottom)

p. 113: © Anne Gummerson

p. 114: © Olson Photographic

p. 115: © Olson Photographic (left); courtesy Mannington (right)

p. 116: courtesy Mannington

p. 117: courtesy *Fine Homebuilding* magazine, © The Taunton Press, Inc. (top); courtesy *Fine Homebuilding* magazine

p. 118: © Tria Giovan (top); © Karen Melvin, design: Martha O'Hara Interiors (bottom left); © Olson Photographic (bottom right)

p. 119: © Karen Melvin, design: Sylvestre Construction

p. 120: © Olson Photographic (left); © Gridley + Graves (right)

p. 121: © Gridley + Graves, architect: Moulton Layne, P.L., www.moultonlayne.com; interior designer: Rod Mickley Interiors, www.rodmickley.com

p. 122: © Ken Gutmaker (left and right)

p. 123: © Randy O'Rourke (top); © Gridley + Graves (bottom)

p. 124: © Olson Photographic (top); © Randy O'Rourke (bottom)

p. 125: © Olson Photographic

p. 126: © Karen Melvin, design: Beret Evenstad Designs, Martha O'Hara Interiors (top); © Anne Gummerson (bottom)

p. 127: © Mark Lohman (left and right)

p. 128: Rob Yagid, courtesy *Fine Homebuilding* magazine, © The Taunton Press, Inc. (left); © Anne Gummerson (right)

p. 129: © Mark Lohman, design: Carolyn Oliver Design

p. 130: © Todd Caverly

p. 131: © Todd Caverly (top); © Greg Hursley (bottom)

pp. 132-133: © Ken Gutmaker (all)

CHAPTER 5

p. 134: © Coles Hairston

p. 136: © Randy O'Rourke (top); © Coles Hairston (bottom)

p. 137: © Todd Caverly (top); © Greg Hursley (bottom)

p. 138: © Todd Caverly (top); © Coles Hairston (bottom left); © Mark Lohman, design: Barclay Butera Inc. (bottom right)

pp. 140-141: © Ken Gutmaker (all)

p. 142: © Mark Lohman, design: Nancy McDonald Design

p. 143: © Todd Caverly

p. 144: © Anne Gummerson

p. 145: © Mark Lohman (top); © Karen Melvin, design: Albertsson Hansen Architecture (bottom)

p. 146: © Olson Photographic

p. 147: © Coles Hairston (top left); © Ken Gutmaker (bottom left); © Randy O'Rourke (right)

p. 148: © Anne Gummerson (top); © Greg Hursley (bottom)

p. 149: © Greg Hursley

p. 150: © Eric Roth (all)

p. 151: © Anne Gummerson (all)

CHAPTER 6

p. 152: Brian Potolilo, courtesy *Fine Homebuilding* magazine, © The Taunton Press, Inc.

p. 154: © Anne Gummerson

p. 155: © Todd Caverly (top); © Greg Hursley (bottom)

pp. 156-157: © Trent Bell (all)

p. 158: © Karen Melvin, design: Sylvestre Construction

p. 159: © Karen Melvin, design: Casa Verde

p. 160: Krysta Doerfler, courtesy *Fine Homebuilding* magazine, © The Taunton Press, Inc. (all)

p. 161: © Greg Hursley (all)

p. 162: © Anne Gummerson

p. 163: Krysta Doerfler, courtesy *Fine Homebuilding* magazine, © The Taunton Press, Inc. (all)

p. 164: courtesy Runtal (top); © Coles Hairston (bottom)

p. 165: courtesy Nuheat Industries (all)

p. 166: © Zach DeSart (all)

CHAPTER 7

p. 168: © Karen Melvin, design: YA Architects

p. 169: © Todd Caverly (top); © Karen Melvin, design: Casa Verde (bottom)

p. 170: © Todd Caverly (top); © Karen Melvin, design: Sylvestre Construction (bottom)

p. 171: © Karen Melvin, design: Merillat Cabinetry (top and bottom)

pp. 172-173: © Greg Auseth (all)

p. 176: © Eric Roth (left); © Anne Gummerson (right)

p. 177: © Karen Melvin (top); © Randy O'Rourke (bottom)

p. 178: © Olson Photographic (top); © Mark Lohman, design: Barclay Butera Inc. (bottom)

p. 179: © Eric Roth (left and right)

p. 180: © Karen Melvin, design: David Heide Design; © Randy O'Rourke (bottom)

p. 181: © Chris Cooper (top); © Karen Melvin, design: YA Architects (bottom)

p. 182: © Tria Giovan

p. 183: © Chris Cooper (top); © Randy O'Rourke (bottom)

p. 184: © Gridley + Graves, design: Craig Kettles, C designs, www.c-designs.biz (top); © Randy O'Rourke (bottom)

p. 185: Brian Urso, courtesy Sharon McCormick Design (top); © Randy O'Rourke (bottom)

p. 186: courtesy Ulrich Inc.

p. 187: © Ken Gutmaker (top left); © Anne Gummerson (bottom left); © Todd Caverly (right)

pp. 188-189: © Greg Auseth (all)

p. 190: © Tria Giovan (top); © Todd Caverly (bottom)

p. 191: © Chris Cooper (left); © Ken Gutmaker (top right); © Mark Lohman (bottom right)

p. 192: © Olson Photographic (top and bottom)

p. 193: © Ken Gutmaker (top left and top right); © Tria Giovan (bottom left and bottom right)

CHAPTER 8

p. 194: © Anne Gummerson

p. 196: © Greg Hursley (top and bottom)

p. 197: © Anne Gummerson (top left); © Chris Cooper (bottom left); © Eric Roth (right)

p. 198: © Anne Gummerson (left); Eric Roth (right)

p. 199: © Anne Gummerson

pp. 200-201: © Greg Auseth (all)

p. 202: © Greg Hursley

p. 203: © Todd Caverly (top left); courtesy Ulrich Inc. (top right); © Anne Gummerson (bottom)

p. 204: © Anne Gummerson (top); © Olson Photographic (bottom)

p. 205: © Anne Gummerson (top); © Eric Roth (bottom left); © Greg Hursley (bottom right)

pp. 206-207: courtesy Ulrich Inc. (all)

p. 208: © Mark Lohman

p. 209: © Mark Lohman (top left and top right); © Tria Giovan (bottom left); © Eric Roth (bottom right)

INDEX

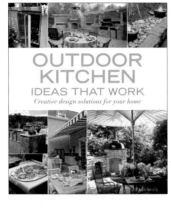
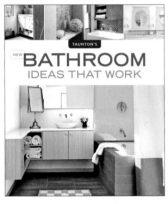